MANY HAPPY RETURNS

MANY

The Viking Press
New York

HAPPY RETURNS

The Art and Sport of Boomeranging

BENJAMIN RUHE

Illustrations by Peter Ruhf

Copyright © Benjamin Ruhe, 1977

First published in 1977 by The Viking Press
625 Madison Avenue, New York, N.Y. 10022

Published simultaneously in Canada by
The Macmillan Company of Canada Limited

LIBRARY OF CONGRESS CATALOGING IN PUBLICATION DATA
Ruhe, Benjamin, 1928-
Many happy returns.
Bibliography: p.
1. Boomerangs.   I. Title.
GV1097.B65R84   799.2'028   76-49837
ISBN 0-670-45412-5

Printed in the United States of America

Set in Photon Highland

Grateful acknowledgment is made to
Little, Brown and Company and Curtis Brown Ltd.:
"Kangaroo" from *Good Intentions* by Ogden Nash.
Copyright 1942 by Ogden Nash.
Reprinted by permission.

ACKNOWLEDGMENTS

This book is respectfully dedicated to those friends and colleagues who have enthusiastically aided the sport of boomeranging.

In the first place, deep appreciation is due Dr. S. Dillon Ripley, Secretary of the Smithsonian Institution. His vision that the National Mall should be more widely used by people directly inspired the development of the sport in Washington.

Contributing their interest in boomeranging in this city and elsewhere around the world were Carolyn Amundson, Dr. Ed Blick, Howard Boys, Leslie Buhler, Bob Coakley, Elizabeth Current, Theresa Cooper, John Daly, Eric Darnell, Vic de Fontenay, Larry Fox, Ali Fujino, Paul Garber, Errol Gautreau, Colonel and Mrs. John Gerrish, Susan Hamilton, Giles Healey, Dr. Felix Hess, Herschel Hurst, MacKenzie Kelly, Dr. Octave Levenspiel, Frank Long, Harry Lowe, Dan Tyler Moore, Dr. Peter Musgrove, Ellen Myette, Carl Naylor, Gordon Rayner, Major Chris Robinson, Cornelius Roosevelt, Barney Ruhe, Captain W. J. Ruhe, Dr. E. L. Ruhe, Peter Ruhf, Steve Silady, Ralph

v

Sinclair, Dr. Harvey Shapiro, Herb Smith, John Strong Sr., Dr. Norman Tindale, Willi Urban, and Mel Zisfein.

For all his valuable collaborative help, deep appreciation is accorded to Dr. Lorin L. Hawes, now Sir Lorin, following his knighthood.

Particular thanks to physicist Dave Robson and anthropologist Errett Callahan. Their keen interest in boomerangs from two quite different vantage points led them to contribute most of the material that appears in Chapters 3 and 9 respectively.

Ann Buchwald and Alida Becker took an idea and made this book come into being. For their vision, expertise, and delight in the project, I thank them.

Finally, Ellen Blue Phillips offered immeasurable help, all of it creative.

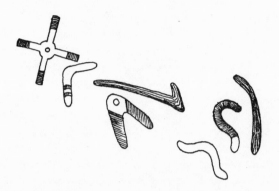

Of all the advantages we have derived from our Australian settlements, none seems to have given more universal satisfaction than the introduction of some crooked pieces of wood shaped like the crescent moon, and called boomerang, or kilee. Ever since their structure has been fully understood, carpenters appear to have ceased from all other work; the windows of toy shops exhibit little else; walking sticks and umbrellas have gone out of fashion; and even in this rainy season no man carries anything but a boomerang; nor does this species of madness appear to be abating.

—*Dublin University Magazine*, February 1838

Boomerangs are more interesting to throw than the javelin and discus, and seem a less outlandish sport than golf.

—Dr. Brenning James, founder of the Society
for the Promotion and Avoidance of Boomerangs

Yes, that's me who worked too much, fifty-five hours in the week. My age is now sixty-eight, but I am throwing the boomerang like the young man . . . sports hold together body and mind.

—Willi Urban, of Leutershausen.
Bavaria, maker of the Comeback boomerang

Oh Kangaroo Oh Kangaroo
Be grateful that you're in the zoo
And not transmuted by a boomerang
To a zestful, tasty Kangaroo meringue

—Ogden Nash

FOREWORD
THE THINKING MAN'S
FRISBEE

The boomerang: a small, curved, wooden stick that returns when you throw it. This is accurate enough as a definition, but sadly inadequate when it comes to describing the charm and challenge of this Stone Age invention.

We live in the Space Age and we have the rocket, a gravity-trapped projectile that follows a simple parabolic curve: launched here, it lands there. The boomerang is more complex: launched here, it lands here. No wonder it is dazzling to scientists. The boomerang provides its own lift and uses its own unique surfaces to change direction. It actually flies.

And it flies with a magical motion. It sails away from you with a fast spin, lifts sharply to the left, and begins to round back. Finding a new direction and spinning some more, it comes back humming and swishing, ending a startling three-dimensional excursion with a brief hover and an obedient descent into your hand.

The boomerang comes from the primitive world of the Australian plain, but fits the temper of our time: partly silly, partly sporting, mildly eccentric, very good exercise. Best of all, it's fun.

CONTENTS

MANY HAPPY RETURNS

IT ALL COMES BACK TO ME NOW

Captain Cook saw his first boomerang at Botany Bay; so did I. The great explorer sighted his "wooden weapons" in 1770, south of Sydney. I had been from Broome in Australia's north to Perth in the west and to Adelaide and Melbourne in the south and not seen any flying boomerangs, although I had watched for them. To me, Australia meant boomerangs just as it meant kangaroos and koala bears and emus and duckbill platypuses. But in 1956 boomerangs were in short supply—that was before jets started bringing tourists to the continent and before Australians learned what visitors wanted to see.

In Sydney, someone told me about an aborigine settlement called La Perouse at Botany Bay where boomerangs were made, flown, and sold to visitors. *Maybe*, if one were lucky and the weather right. So following instructions, I took an old trolley south to the end of the line—La Perouse. As I got off the train, I saw flashes in the sky above a nearby hillside. Boomerangs! Half-a-dozen young aborigines—half-castes, I learned later—were there in a rocky field, throwing and catching boomerangs and clearly having a great time of it. They were happy to see me, naturally, and one of them sold me the best performer he had. He showed me how to throw it, and when I let loose, the boomerang made a lovely free circle in the air, came spinning back, made a second small circle, and landed close by. It acted like a bird, dipping up and down in response to air currents as it spun around, whirring faintly like a miniature helicopter. In the air it had a personality and sound all its own.

My first boomerang was of hardwood, finely crafted; the next two purchases were plywood models, less well made but also less breakable. These were all the boys would sell me.

They were enough to satisfy me. On the way back to Sydney I happily clutched my three returning boomerangs —I had hunted long and hard for them, and they had all the charm of a childhood dream.

Australia was the final stop on my two-year vagabond walkabout. I'd paid for it by building houses in France, cutting trails for cows at a Swiss students' work camp, living on the monastery peninsula of Mount Athos in Greece, and studying religion at an Indian village devoted to Gandhian principles. In the Himalayas I appeared before royalty—the kings of Hunza and Nagir—in the western Karakorams below Sinkiang, where there were twenty-five-thousand-foot mountains, some of which were still unclimbed. I went to Hunza by invitation: the king and I had a mutual friend, the organic foods prophet J. I. Rodale. Once there, I received an invitation from the King of Nagir, who was jealous that his rival had company. I accepted and a few days later trudged across a foaming river and along some rough Himalayan terrain with a knapsack on my back. Waiting for me at the Nagir border were courtiers on horseback, pennants flying from their lances. They were my escort to the palace. That mountain jaunt, straight out of the Middle Ages, was soon over, and it was back to tramping for me.

Several months and thousands of miles later I was in

Australia, and my funds were low. After a lot of job-hunting, an employment agency shipped me 400 miles by train up into the northeast corner of New South Wales. The Kenniff family of Boggabri needed a jackaroo-cowboy, gardener, and handyman on their big sheep and cattle station. Kevin Kenniff hired me despite his reservations about my competence. I had come a long way and was an American, a member of the nation that had saved his country from the Japanese during World War II (such was the Australian attitude). But his doubts about my ability soon proved well founded. I couldn't ride a horse.

However, that didn't stop me from getting aboard the smart old mare the station provided from its herd of semi-wild steeds. It turned out to be a viable partnership: she did the herding; I hung on.

For the next several months, we moved flocks of sheep, coaxed the cattle on to greener pastures, and for sport, chased kangaroos across the arid plain. In addition to galloping about, I watered the garden, milked the lone cow, plowed some fields for wheat, and did odd jobs when a team of sheepshearers came around to do their annual task. Lucky for my ears that the profane rhyming slang of the Australians is almost incomprehensible to outsiders.

Evenings, after eating mutton cooked by my fellow ranch hand, who simply threw a slab of raw meat on a red-hot cookstove, I threw boomerangs. Cockatoos and kookaburras watched from the trees. When they flew past, I threw boomerangs at them. They dodged.

The way I was going, it would have been years before I saved passage money back to America. Australia's tropic north, with lovely Pacific islands just beyond, beckoned with the easy life. My letters reflected this and my father sent me a loan, suggesting I come home. I went; it was then or never.

Work; drab routines of adult life; boomerangs broken; Australia almost forgotten.

Then one spring day in 1969, I happened to take a walk across the National Mall in Washington with Susan Hamilton, a fellow staff member at the Smithsonian Institution.

3

Susan was director of the Smithsonian Resident Associates, a membership group formed to develop a variety of new and interesting programs, and we were talking about Secretary S. Dillon Ripley's plans to bring more people to the huge, empty Mall. Susan's Associates group had just sponsored an immensely popular kite carnival at the Washington Monument. "Why not a boomerang throw-in?" I suggested, more as a joke than anything else. "Let's do it," said Susan. "Right away."

So I dug out the old broken boomerangs I had never repaired, figured out how to make new ones, sent dozens of letters around the world soliciting information and help, and planned a workshop for the making and throwing of boomerangs.

The sport caught on immediately, partly because of Smithsonian prestige and partly because of expanding interest in folk, ethnic, and primitive lore. The Frisbee was a factor—the boomerang has a lot of the same elements that make the Frisbee so popular.

Refinements in Australian boomerang design helped, too. Instead of big, heavy, dangerous objects, we could now get small, light, delicate, finely crafted boomerangs. Anyone with a reasonable arm could make them perform in five minutes flat. And the designs were easy to copy. One man in our first workshop shaped a light model with hand tools, then went out with the group to try his results. On his first toss, the boomerang came exactly back and whacked him on the forehead. He was delighted.

Since we were Americans, there was no alternative but to have a competition following the first workshop, and this, too, was a success. There wasn't much competition, but it was a lot of fun. Thus began the annual Smithsonian boomerang corroboree on the Mall. It's been a pleasure to many, a joke to some, a source of anecdote and of much publicity to all—what might be called (with apologies) a booming success.

Actually, boomeranging is not a sport for big tournaments at all. It's for the knowledgeable few, for several friends who get together and throw to their heart's content without anyone else around. Spectators are distracting; besides, they might get hit by an errant boomerang.

It definitely is a sport for adventuresome people; it's something different that's fun to do, fun to talk about, and attracts gratifying attention. The impact in Washington has been considerable, and a national ripple effect can be discerned if you look hard enough.

The aftermath of the Washington tournament indicates how quickly a boomerang fad can develop. Avid throwers were Dick Helms and his wife Cynthia (he was at that time Director of the CIA and she was a Smithsonian staff member). Ben Bradlee, who supervised *The Washington Post*'s Watergate investigation, kept one of my boomerangs on his desk. Martha Mitchell wrote me to ask for a private lesson for her daughter, but then called it off when her personal publicity became too intense. Dr. Ripley, the august secretary of the Smithsonian, once approached me at a party to talk boomerangs and ended up asking for a lesson outside his office in the Smithsonian Castle.

Carpenters from the Smithsonian's National Museum of Natural History learned to make their own boomerangs and took to throwing them at lunch. The high-intelligence group, Mensa, staged its own tournament. Programmers at a suburban Washington defense center set up an afternoon throwing club. As a crafts project, a school in Arlington, Virginia, encouraged its pupils to make and throw boomerangs.

As the resident Smithsonian boomerang freak, I've designed a boomerang exhibit for the giant new National Air and Space Museum. I've lectured before scout troops, summer camps, schools, Goddard Space Flight Center scientists, and to the International Platform Association. In a coals-to-Newcastle turnabout, I've even lectured at the Australian Embassy.

Boomerangs get attention. Low-flying helicopters alter their flights to get a look at the strange goings-on below. Birds flying past a boomerangfest often drop down to examine the missiles; sometimes they follow a boomerang right around its circle. In the most curious of these avian incidents, a small bird rose out of the grass to attack a boomerang flying over her. She did this repeatedly, probably defending her nest. Unfortunately, when a film team came out to record the phenomenon, the brave little bird did not appear.

Mass boomerang throws amaze tourists, particularly Australians. One Aussie came tearing across the Mall to see if his eyes were deceiving him. "What's going on here? Boomerangs are Australian!" was his reaction. When told it was a tournament, he was nonplussed. "Mad Yanks!" he said.

The ripples of all this activity have spread quite a distance:

In Baltimore, a high school teacher named David Robson developed a science course he calls "Birds, Boeings, and Boomerangs." Students who can't master the aerodynamic principles that are part of the requirements still get credit for good throws.

Physicist Martin Olsson, having taken up boomerangs as a subject in his studies, discovered that his boomerang orbited thirty yards in Madison, Wisconsin, but had an orbit diameter of fifty yards in Aspen, Colorado, where at 8,000 feet the air is thin. A physicist in San Diego, Gordon Rayner, introduced boomerang throwing to the nude bathing scene in California. Rayner, who was, in his own words, wearing "authentic aboriginal costume—pre-missionary," documented his laudable enterprise with color photographs.

Bob Jensen acquired boomerangs from me and later reported throwing them from fissures in Yosemite and from lava beds in McKenzie Pass, Oregon. "How's that for madness?" he asked.

Erroll Gautreau organized a club in Baton Rouge, Louisiana, called the Ruhe-Rang-ers, first asking permission to use my name, which I gave with some amazement.

Stewart Brand, California guru of the youth culture, ran portions of the Smithsonian's boomerang booklet, including a construction plan, in his *Whole Earth Catalog*, thereby making possible the creation of thousands of boomerangs all over the world.

Boomeranging even made some people wax poetic. One was a deft left-handed thrower named Christopher Ruhe, a folk singer by trade and a nephew of mine, who penned this verse:

> *through the aural space*
> *of a red and yellow*
> *October dusk*
> *sings the boomerang . . .*
> *cutting the cool air . . .*
> *a trail of spirit heat*
> *leaving.*

Dr. Harvey Shapiro, a psychiatrist from Portland, Oregon, put *his* personal feelings into medical language after receiving some fine boomerangs. "Ever since last Sunday," he wrote, "I have been in an acute, fulminating attack of my chronic boomerangosis." Dr. John Greenway, a Colorado anthropologist, said he received a boomerang but didn't know whether it worked or not. He gave it away before having tried to use it. "It didn't come back," he complained.

The boomerang's time has come, it seems. In England, Dr. Brennig James organized The Society for the Promotion and Avoidance of Boomerangs; his prior claim to fame was a solo ascent to 26,000 feet in a sailplane, clad in swimming trunks. Dr. James later threw boomerangs from Himalayan peaks, claiming high-altitude records.

In Holland, Felix Hess conducted the most profound studies yet on the boomerang. Using a computer, he was able to project imaginary boomerang flights. When he sent along some printouts, I told him they were beautiful examples of conceptual art. The next ones I received were signed. Concluding seven years of study, Hess earned his

7

doctorate at the University of Groningen with a dissertation on the boomerang. His scholarship adds a certain seriousness to the sport.

Also in the Netherlands, Max Hoeben, of Amstelveen, runs tournaments and manufactures balsa-wood boomerangs that invalids can throw in a hall. They use a magnet mounted on a stick to catch the boomerangs in midair.

Nationally subsidized boomeranging is reported from France; and Willi Urban of Leutershausen tells me that throwing boomerangs is a growing sport in Germany too.

Of course, I spread the word by sending boomerangs as presents to friends in many countries: South Africa, Rhodesia, India, Brazil, Honduras, Egypt, Russia, Sweden. The Swede, from Malmö, told me he wanted to return the favor, but that there were only two things of good value available to him—clogs, "too uncomfortable for the feet," he decided, and pornographic movies. One of the latter arrived three months after our discussion, packed in a sack of camomile tea. The film was very blue indeed.

Leroy Woodson, a *National Geographic* photographer, took a number of boomerangs with him when he went to photograph Kurds in Iraq and gave them to the children. An ethnologist who heard of this said: "He shouldn't have done that. It will mess up their culture."

In Australia, the motherland, boomeranging is now big business. Tourists demand to see kangaroos, wallabies, wombats, duckbill platypuses, and boomerangs; and the Australians oblige. Natives—white and brown—have learned how to make boomerangs for the tourist trade, have discovered in the process that throwing is fun, and have made it a small institution. Now there are city and national associations tournaments—prizes well worth winning. The game has acquired semi-professional overtones, and Australians even talk of introducing boomerang-throwing as an Olympic sport.

If the whole subject is beginning to sound more serious than it ought to be, consider the opinion of Mark Twain, who saw boomerangs in Australia in 1897. "Either some-one with a boomerang arrived in Australia in the days of antiquity," he wrote, "or the Australian aborigines re-invented it. It will take some time to find out which of these two propositions is the fact. But there is no hurry."

PREHISTORIC AERONAUTICS

How in the world did the boomerang ever come to be invented? It's been said that if you fully understand the
sophisticated principles governing the flight of this device,
there is nothing in aeronautics and astronautics you won't
understand. Yet the men who made it were the most primitive of humans. How did they do it? And when? And
where, exactly?

These are difficult questions. But we now have masses of
information, some of it misinformation to be sure, gathered
over almost 200 years. We can make some educated
guesses. And as young scientists enter the field, we learn
more and more on the subject. So let's plunge in.

The aborigines of Australia are among the most archaic of
men, physically quite close to Neanderthal man. They have
only one domestic animal, the dingo, a kind of dog. They
neither farm nor garden; instead, they roam a vast territory
of inhospitable prairie and desert eking out a meager exist-

ence; grubs, ants, and seeds are prominent fare. They have few material possessions, all of which are carried by hand, as the people do "walkabouts" across the hundreds of miles of their territory.

Yet these mostly naked, brown wanderers developed and used the returning boomerang, a curved stick that flies like a bird and returns unerringly to the hands of its thrower. And they apparently had it for many centuries. We know how other aboriginal peoples invented and perfected certain weapons, and we know there has been no genetic change in mankind in ten thousand years; it is logical that what feels right to us would have felt comfortable to men of the Ice Age. We can speculate, therefore, about how the boomerang came into being. We can argue about alternative theories.

Nearly everyone interested in the matter agrees on some version of the evolution theory. For several complicated reasons, the boomerang is a device that returns, and the trick in tracing its development is to guess how the necessary aerodynamics evolved as man produced tools to cope with his environment.

Stone Age man bagged game by throwing things at it— rocks, boulders, tree limbs, whatever was handy. Throwing made him effective at a distance. Eventually, he produced the club for throwing, which later developed into a thinned-down curved weapon. When it was thrown, it flew long and straight. The curve of the weapon kept it stabilized in flight and enabled it to spin for a longer period than a straight stick; its lighter weight permitted it to be thrown with more speed; and its thinned-down shape provided a rude airfoil and afforded lift to the device. It could *fly*. The throw stick, as this thinned-down weapon is known, was not only an effective weapon for hunting and war, but also possessed the essential elements that, refined and slightly modified, almost certainly led to the boomerang.

Before taking up the boomerang, it is important to examine this throw stick in some detail, both because it's interesting in its own right, and because, as the probable parent of the boomerang, it must be understood thoroughly before one takes the next step in analyzing the famous comeback device.

The typical throw stick is about three feet long and is curved like a banana; it has a wing three inches across, and a tear-shaped cross section a half-inch thick. It weighs a pound or less. When thrown, it sails low to the ground and fairly straight. If the flight path is slightly curved, the aborigine hunter programs that into his aim.

Apparently a rather universal fighting weapon and hunting device, the throw stick has been found in ancient Egypt, South India, North Africa, and prehistoric Europe. Various names are applied to it in addition to throw stick: straight-flying stick, rabbit stick, hunting boomerang, killer boomerang, and fighting boomerang are some of those names. The word "boomerang" creeps in through a confusion. Even though the throw stick doesn't return, it is often called a boomerang because when the British settled coastal New South Wales almost two centuries ago, they applied the word indiscriminately to both the non-returning and returning wooden objects in use—they probably heard the vanished Tharawal and Daruk tribes of New South Wales describing their curved wooden throwing devices as "bou-ma-rang."

The word "boomerang" was used by the English throughout Australia, even though the aborigines themselves had more than three hundred names for the two devices, such as *nanjal, baranganj, kali,* and *wilgi.* Two of my favorites are *barngeet* and *tootgundy.*

The throw stick was widely used throughout Australia and in many other places around the world. In some regions it was undoubtedly replaced by the more efficient bow and arrow. The throw stick hangs on, though, in places where it works best: semi-arid plains with few trees or bushes to impede its flight. It was probably independently invented in a

12

number of regions of the world.

Indians of the American southwest, such as the Hopi, have the throw stick; they called it a rabbit stick because it was used both to hit rabbits on the run and to club them to death during rabbit drives. These throw sticks are of ancient origin; the pre-Columbian ancestors of the Hopi, the Anasazi, also used them.

Of the many regions outside Australia where the throw stick was used, ancient Egypt is by far the most interesting to study. First-rate specimens from the burial sites are preserved in museums, and their use is documented in wall paintings found in some of those tombs. One such mural, a reproduction of which is in the collection of the Metropolitan Museum of Art in New York, shows *Menna, the Scribe of the Fields*, using a throw stick to hunt flying waterfowl. Throw sticks have been found from the Sixth, Eleventh, and Eighteenth Dynasties, among others, dating them back in time at least 4,300 years.

Photographs of throw sticks found in the tomb of Tutankhamen were published by the English archaeologist Howard Carter, whose tomb discoveries in the 1920s startled the world. Some of these throw sticks are spectacular, made of ivory with gold caps and elaborate colored engravings. Carter believed that throw sticks were used in Egypt from the earliest to the last dynasties; he also believed that the throw stick was employed in warfare, and that the device used by the nobility for fowling in the swamps of the Nile was a *returning* boomerang.

Seemingly not as impressive and complicated as some other weapons, the throw stick was nevertheless efficient enough when compared with bow and arrow, spear, sling, bola, blowgun, throwing knife, and other early projectile weapons. It had advantages all its own.

Ballistically, for example, the throw stick is more advanced. Rocks, sticks, spears, and arrows follow a parabolic arc as their flight trajectory; they are pulled to earth by gravity. If any great distance is involved, all must be aimed high when thrown. The throw stick, on the other hand, partly defies gravity; it has its own lift, so it planes. It skims the ground and can be aimed directly at the quarry —a great advantage. Moreover, it goes an exceptional distance.

Although primitive man customarily creeps close to his game if at all possible, he obviously can't get very close to it on treeless plains. Errett Callahan, of Richmond, Virginia has illustrated this crucial potential for long-distance throwing. He can hurl a throw stick approximately 170 yards, but can throw a club of similar weight only 54 yards —with a throw stick, he triples his distance.

The throw stick has a final advantage—a broad sweep. Instead of having to be aimed precisely like a dart or a stone hurled from a sling, it cuts a deadly three-foot swath. This is clearly advantageous to a hungry hunter.

Unlike many primitive weapons, the throw stick takes effect by stunning, breaking bones, and maiming, though on occasion it may cut like a throwing knife or pierce like an arrow. One Australian aborigine adversary in a nineteenth-century quarrel was killed when a throw stick struck his chest point first and passed completely through his body. More recently, a police trooper in central Australia was killed by a thrown boomerang while trying to halt a fight between an aborigine man and woman.

Ethnographic literature on Australia is, in fact, replete with accounts of the deadliness of the weapon, and it is not hard to believe these bloody accounts. Because of its spin, a big throw stick at the end of its flight will easily take up a large divot or hunk of turf. Think of having a golf club swung at you! That's what being hit with a throw stick would feel like.

The product of a culture of few materials, the throw stick had many uses aside from that of an object to be thrown. (This holds true for the boomerang too, of course.) It can become a battle club or it can stun and kill a wounded animal. The sharpened tip at one end is used to cut open and chop up kangaroos and other game—or lever tendons out of animal carcasses for use as bindings.

The throw stick can be used to dig wells and fire-sites, to unearth honey ants and lizards, to scrape hot ashes from baked emus in the fire, and to sharpen flint tools by striking flakes from them. Used as a friction saw on softwood, the throw stick creates sparks, and these are caught in tinder to make fire. Used as a bow, the boomerang is rubbed across the edge of another boomerang to make a curious musical sound; two of them rapidly tapped together make a percussive clattering; beating one of them on the earth makes a rhythmic thud; whirled over the head, a boomerang creates yet another kind of musical noise. Uses extend to the ridiculous: an aborigine was once seen cleaning his teeth with his boomerang.

clacking

The many uses of the throw stick were important for a semi-nomadic people who were forced to roam great distances seeking food in a hostile environment: they faced a glaring sun by day, a chill breeze by night, and a general scarcity of water. They needed the freedom of movement afforded by a multipurpose implement they could carry by

15

hand. Remember that these were people without metals, pottery, bows and arrows, or agriculture.

So much for the throw stick. Now we turn to the boomerang, the stick that returns.

Remember that the throw stick, almost certainly the parent of the boomerang, had elements that, with refining and modification, logically could have led to the development of the comeback model. These elements are a curve (to keep the instrument spinning longer), light enough weight so the stick could be thrown quite hard and with a lot of wrist snap, and wings with a kind of teardrop shape to provide aerodynamic lift.

At this point we are almost forced to think in terms of personal genius, the quantum leap of the man who, with luck and insight, makes a great discovery. Imagine an aborigine accidentally crafting a throw stick a bit lighter than usual, one with a sharper curve than usual, and suppose the surfaces are just right—the bottom side is flat, or nearly so, and the top side is curved. Suppose he throws this creation, and it curves around quite sharply and— perhaps blown by the wind—comes almost back to him. The aboriginal hunter is charmed, as we would be charmed. Joined by fellow hunters, he throws and throws and learns the best launch angle and how to use the wind to his advantage. His friends copy his invention, and some of them get even more favorable dimensions and obtain even better flights. They incorporate the new invention into their hunting and into their rituals. The returning boomerang has been born. Believable? I don't see why not.

But as I said, there are other theories on how the boomerang came into being:

In a version of the evolution hypothesis stated earlier, Dr. Peter Musgrove, a scientist from the University of Reading in England, puts forth the wooden sword theory. Along with just about everyone else, Peter believes aboriginal man didn't have to sit down and conceive the fin-

16

ished product before he carved his first boomerang. The process, he believes, started with rounded clubs that evolved into thinned-down slashing ones. Curving the wooden blade like a scimitar would intensify the cutting effect. Peter than offers a pretty image—a swordsman hurls his wooden scimitar at a retreating enemy and the weapon takes effect at a distance. The thrower is surprised at how far the weapon travels and at its slightly curved flight. Experiments reveal how to accentuate the length and curve of the flight. Eventually, the returning boomerang is born. The beauty of this hypothesis, as Dr. Musgrove points out, is that it doesn't demand a conceptual breakthrough on the part of the aborigine.

Now for a theory with charm. Have you ever seen how leaves and seed pods sail in the autumn? Australia is the home of the eucalyptus, or gum tree. A leaf from this tree, if thrown forward, makes a curve and comes right back. A man watching children play with such leaves might have been prompted to make a leaf model out of wood to please them. Its peculiar performance could have led to experiments by the man and his friends, and eventually the boomerang could have come into being. Not convinced? Neither am I.

Let's try the propellor theory. A throw stick becomes wet from the dew, or from landing in some water, and warps. One wing tip bends up a bit, the opposite one down. Looking at this object lengthwise, one sees its propellor shape. If weight, curve, and other factors are favorable, such a throw stick might curve around sharply. More twist, and it returns. The boomerang is born.

Note that warping is a kind of red-herring issue. A returning boomerang is not necessarily warped, but warping can sometimes make a boomerang return. It was long thought, by the way, that twisting was the secret to the returning boomerang's performance, and this analysis is duly given in much nineteenth-century literature. It's simply not true. One Englishman, Sir Thomas Mitchell, *did* invent a new kind of screw propellor in 1846 on the basis of his observations of the twist in aboriginal boomerangs, so one good thing did come of the theory. But I, for one, want to set the question of warping and twisting pretty much aside, because it just complicates an already complex subject.

Now, for my favorite theory. Vic de Fontenay, a date palm grower in Alice Springs, Australia, is apparently the originator of this hypothesis, and he is the one who brought the theory to my attention. Vic noticed that some of his date palm stems were shaped like returning boomerangs; he speculated that the date palm was not indigenous to Australia. If date palm stems could be made to behave as boomerangs in tests, it might not be outlandish to theorize that the returning boomerang originated in countries where the date palm grew—perhaps the Tigris-Euphrates basin. De Fontenay sent me some of his stems, after having had a lot of trouble fumigating them so the U.S. government would let them in. When I went to Dulles Airport, near Washington, one night to pick up the shipment, everyone at the Trans World Airlines air cargo depot was eagerly waiting for me. The package was conspicuously labeled: *Boomerangs, for scientific study by the Smithsonian Institution.*

"What are you going to kill with them?" asked one man as I cut the box open.

"They're supposed to be returning boomerangs," said a friend of mine who had come along, "and returning boomerangs are used for play."

"Can't you kill anything with them?"

"No."

"Oh." Disappointment.

The date palm stems indeed had the right shape and weight, and I took the best of them to a field next day. On the first test flight, the three-foot stem curved to the right —wrong direction. I twisted it a bit, and it went straight. I twisted it some more, and it curved to the left. Twisted a bit more, the curve was even sharper.

The date palm is fibrous and strong, so in order to twist it more, I had to take the stem home, soak and bake it. But I did achieve return flights, with some help from the wind, and it was something of a triumph. Notice here that the success does not completely prove the point, since I already knew what kind of flight pattern was needed and how to bend the stem to achieve it. But since we're talking in terms of tens of thousands of years, there seems no reason why one date palm stem somewhere at some time could not have had just the right shape, and when picked up and hurled at a flock of birds could not have come boomeranging back. A chauvinist chorus from Australia replies here, "We believe you, thousands wouldn't."

If you accept this hypothesis, you've somehow got to get the boomerang to Australia. De Fontenay theorizes that aboriginal peoples in the Tigris-Euphrates basin would have exported it to neighbors or carried it in migrations. When the boomerang reached lands where date palms did not grow, the device would have been duplicated in available hardwoods.

That's the theory. I've tried it out on a number of Australians, and it tends to enrage them. "Boomerangs are Australian [it came out "*Strine*"]!" I'm not really prepared to fight over the matter. Punch-ups, as anyone knows, are one of the Australian national sports.

Now for another question. How old is the boomerang?

Rock paintings in Australia known to be quite old—perhaps thousands of years—depict throw sticks and boomerangs; but the age of this art is impossible to determine precisely. A recent discovery by a young American scientist, Roger Leubbers, is important because what appear to be boomerangs found by him and his group can actually be dated by the radiocarbon 14 process. Digging in Wyrie Swamp, near Lake Bonny, 220 miles southwest of Adelaide, Leubbers unearthed wood fragments in a peat bog that are estimated to range from 11,000 to 15,000 years in age. The former date comes from a layer just above that in which the fragments were found; the latter is known to be the earliest time the bog existed.

What's fascinating about the find is that the objects can be presumed to be returning boomerangs and not just throw sticks. The reasoning is that aborigines might have developed the comeback boomerang when they hunted over marshes, tidelands, or swamps, where retrieval would have been difficult or impossible. It was, after all, hard work making a wooden implement with stone tools, and aboriginal peoples who did this probably would have valued the objects they so arduously created. Besides, a good boomerang would be valued for itself as a kind of magical device, and it would not be casually lost. Given my own attachment to certain boomerangs, I don't find it hard to imagine aboriginal devotion to a particularly efficient game-getter.

Leubbers' discovery could place the known age of Australian returning boomerangs far back in time. But there's no reason to believe other swamps don't contain even older samples. Archaeological dates are being pushed farther back in time every year.

A question now presents itself: is the boomerang known only to Australia? If not, where else did it exist?

Because it is a national symbol, the boomerang is increasingly valued by Australians. If I were an Aussie, I too would claim the boomerang as a unique down under invention. But just as the kangaroo and wallaby have their marsupial relatives in America, so the returning boomerang may have a counterpart elsewhere in the world. The evidence for this is growing. As one example, physicist Felix Hess reproduced in plywood as closely as he could (and being a scientist he's a careful man) a boomerang-like object of oak dug up in three pieces in 1962 at an Iron Age site near Velsen, on the Dutch coast. The find dated to 2300 years before the present. The boomerang has an angle between its arms of 110 degrees; one side is convex, and the other side flat. All are favorable specifications. Dr. Hess emphasizes that his copy is just that, a copy, and acknowledges that the warping is perhaps different from the original. When he threw it in 1974, his model went outward about twenty-four yards, curved around, and returned nicely to him. The flight lasted about seven seconds. In an article describing the experiment in *Antiquity*, the archaeological review of St. John's College, Cambridge, he claims, "This appears to be the first instance in which a boomerang of non-Australian origin is shown to be returning."

Others before him have also suspected finding returning boomerangs outside Australia. Mr. I. Edwards, keeper of Egyptian antiquities at the British Museum, cites as an example the former director of the Cairo Museum, a man named Engleback, who obtained some copies of boomerangs in the museum's collection and threw them "so they returned in a regular manner." The only person who saw him throw his copies of tomb boomerangs, apparently made for him by the museum carpenter, was the late Professor Newberry, who had a file of information on the subject he bequeathed to a library; his notes were subsequently thought worthless and were destroyed.

All's not lost though. An Oxford scholar, Vivian Davies, has access to the university's archaeological materials and is studying Egyptian tomb weapons. He points out that a throw stick illustrated in Howard Carter's book *The Tomb of Tutankhamen* is made of hardwood, has a skew to the wing tips that might help make it return, and has some other characteristics of the returning boomerang. Studies are proceeding; replicas will no doubt be made and actual field experiments will be conducted.

Norman Tindale, the distinguished Australian anthropologist-archaeologist who has generously shared the insights from his fifty years of field research with me, feels sure returning boomerangs were used elsewhere in the world. He bases his heretical (for an Australian) supposition on the same form-follows-function argument cited by Roger Leubbers in his swamp finds: where primitive peoples hunted flocks of birds over water, tidelands, or marshes, they would have inevitably developed throw sticks that returned.

Dr. Tindale's view is not to be taken lightly. His knowledge of aboriginal men and their manner of life is so profound it often astonishes his peers. Once, for example, on a visit to the University of Kansas, he went scouting for Indian sites with his host professors and so startled them with his ability to pick out camp grounds unnoticed by the others that he was offered an exchange professorship almost on the spot.

We get to firmer ground with the next inquiry. What was the function of returning boomerangs? A number of uses are known, and others can be safely imagined.

Boomerangs were certainly used for play, for pure sport, and for fun. As a charming amusement in Queensland, a live coal was attached to a returning boomerang, which was hurled aloft at night to spin through the dark sky as a kind of primitive Fourth of July sparkler.

One aborigine competition tested which man could make his boomerang accomplish the greatest number of circles and return closest to the point of launching, or could return to a peg hammered into the ground. In one region, a game consisted of throwing a boomerang and trying to make it strike a peg on its return.

A curious game is described by one nineteenth-century observer. Half-a-dozen Australian aboriginal men stood Indian file, each resting his hands on the shoulders of the one in front. A thrower positioned himself some distance ahead and, facing the file, tossed a boomerang over their heads. As the boomerang circled around and swooped down, each man in the file tried to dodge it. If he didn't, too bad for him. (I've been hit by big boomerangs, and it hurts.) Each man got a chance to throw, turn and turn about.

Returning boomerangs were used in certain kinds of hunting. Throwing at dense flocks of birds was common, and several birds might be crippled and knocked down by one implement. Aborigines typically launched two or three boomerangs in rapid succession at birds flying past; or two or three men threw all at once.

If a boomerang thrown at a bird dealt the quarry just a glancing blow, the boomerang might well return almost on plan. A solid hit would probably stop the boomerang cold, not to mention the duck; some wading was then in store for the hunter. But with meat to retrieve, he probably wouldn't mind.

Dr. Tindale describes an interesting use of boomerangs in hunting. Nets made of fiber string prepared by chewing plant roots were hung across a narrow stretch of water or over a flyway between lakes. When a flight of water birds was sighted, hunters imitated the cry of a hawk and threw a boomerang high into the air to represent the bird of prey. Alarmed, the birds flew quite low—right into the nets. Waiting men pulled the trap tight, and the hunt was over.

Returning boomerangs, however, weren't ordinarily used for hunting animals on the ground, since they soar too high while in flight. Throw sticks were employed instead.

It's probably safe to say that in a primitive society such as that of the Australian aborigines, every object possessed has a sacred aspect, or can be given one at times of ceremony. Throw sticks and boomerangs thus had another important use—in ritual.

Unusual cross-stick boomerangs were used in a dance by the Kunggandyi tribe of Cairns, Queensland. These returning boomerangs, called "pirbu pirbu" (the only boomerangs known in Australia that do not conform to the usual bi-wing shape), were twirled by means of a stick fastened in the back to simulate the boomerang spinning through the air. This was done in a rhythmic movement as the dancers shuffled around in a circle.

In the Cooper's Creek area, aborigines showed off for each other by carving and prominently displaying "prestige" throw sticks. These creations were perfect in every detail, but were so big they couldn't be thrown. Any aborigine with any pretension had one displayed outside his campsite. Some of these boomerangs are said to have approached an impressive twelve feet in height.

Here's another curiosity, probably with ritualistic meaning: throw sticks and boomerangs often are manufactured, used, and even traded as pairs. An aborigine may have one spear, one shield, and one of a number of other devices, such as digging sticks or bark-collecting bowls for witchetty grubs, yet he will carry two boomerangs. This custom remains unexplained.

The swan-necked throw stick from the Northern Territory is one of the most beautiful of all aboriginal creations; it is also referred to as the hooked, the horned, or the beaked throw stick. Its shape is the normal shallow curve of the throw stick, except that, as the names imply, a beak-like projection extends abruptly out from one tip for no explainable reason. One theory has it that the projection hooked on to a shield and permitted the weapon to lash around into the enemy, trying to ward it off. The beak may, on the other hand, simply be a wooden equivalent of a stone pick for close-quarter battling. It may serve only a decorative function.

Some throw sticks and boomerangs have a curious longitudinal fluting on the upper or curved side. The purpose of this is not known. By causing a disturbance of the air on the upper side of the missile, the fluting may give the device lift, as the dimples in a golf ball give the ball lift and provide greater range. On the other hand, the fluting may simply be decoration. Adding this fluting, incidentally, is a test of skill. Gripping the boomerang under the heel, the aboriginal craftsman uses a stone-tipped chisel and starts at one end, working down to the middle. Then he reverses the procedure and cuts grooves from the other direction. Good craftsman that he is, these grooves meet exactly in the middle. And he doesn't nick his legs or feet once.

People assume that returning boomerangs as well as non-returning throw sticks were known everywhere in Australia. In fact, returning boomerangs were always rare and highly prized on that continent. Tribes who knew how to fashion them sometimes traded them to tribes who didn't have this knowledge. Boomerangs were unknown in the far north and along a broad swath cutting down into the middle of Australia. Throw sticks were more widely distributed but were also unknown in the north and in a large patch of desert in the lower center of the continent.

Because migration into Australia probably came from the extreme north, where there was once a land bridge to Asia, this distribution of both boomerangs and throw sticks suggests the invention of both devices by the Australian aborigines. Mr. de Fontenay's date-palm-stem theory is thus discredited, unless the migrations he envisions occurred very far back in time and involved an earlier flow of people than is known to us.

As I said before, twisting and bending constitute a red herring problem with boomerangs. A boomerang returns perfectly well without any warping, yet many aboriginal boomerangs are warped; the nineteenth-century students of the boomerang assumed they had found the secret of the returning boomerang when they analyzed the warping and what it could achieve. The twist we're talking about is a two- to four-degree upward skew in either wing tip. Bending the leading edge of the wing tip tends to make the boomerang return; bending it down tends to make the boomerang fly straight.

Aborigines are quite aware of this technique; in some places they use it to convert a returner into a non-returner, or vice versa, as the day's activities dictate. Thus we have the ultimate complexity—a returning boomerang made within minutes into a nonreturning throw stick, or the other way around. Dr. Tindale says he has seen this trimming done many times. As he explained to me in a letter: "[Aborigines] habitually rewarp their boomerangs to perform whichever function is for the moment uppermost in their minds. Setting a boomerang is, one might say, a daily chore when hunting is a prospect, or when a game is to be played in making their weapon return. Primary and secondary uses determine the degree of warp that is desirable at the time."

The famous carved wooden stick of the Australian aborigine is a war weapon one day, an object for sport the next, a ceremonial implement the third. Meanwhile, it can be used to dig, to create music, to act as a lever, to knap flints, to cleave various objects, or to make fire. It's a wonderfully useful invention.

So the next time you see an aboriginal boomerang in a museum and think of it as a relic of the simple-minded Stone Age, reflect a bit.

THE REASONS WHY

The boomerang is a simple mechanical device with one moving part that performs a surprising feat. It boomerangs, or returns. As children, we learned that a thrown rattle, rock, or baseball keeps moving away. The boomerang, an inanimate piece of wood, fails to behave in this manner. Unseen forces are clearly at work, but what are they?

Explanations of this phenomenon first began in the nineteenth century; yet the boomerang still remains a puzzle to almost everyone. Why? Although the problem appears quite simple, it is actually quite complex. A number of scientific rules are obeyed by the boomerang as it traces a circle in the sky. Are you ready? They include Bernoulli's principle, Newton's laws of motion, gyroscopic stability, and gyroscopic precession. Few mechanical devices demonstrate so many laws working together, and this gives the impression that the boomerang follows *no* law.

Briefly stated, the boomerang returns because (a) its wings generate lift; (b) the spin imparted to the device makes it act like a gyroscope and thus gives it stability in the air; and (c) the spin and forward motion make it turn because of the phenomenon called gyroscopic precession.

We'll examine these concepts in an elementary way, with the help of drawings. If the scientific principles governing boomerangs intrigue you, you might want to consult some of the weightier accounts cited in the bibliography. If, however, you feel like getting on with boomerang making and throwing, make a mental note to come back and study the aerodynamics when you can. It may destroy the mystery of the boomerang for you, but on the other hand you'll almost certainly be the only one on your block who can explain to his friends—physicists included—why a boomerang actually boomerangs.

We begin by examining the device itself. Each arm is shaped like the wing of an airplane, with a flat side and a curved side. Like the airplane wing, the spinning arms of the boomerang will produce a lifting force in the direction of the curved surface. This would suggest that the boomerang should be thrown sidearm to give it a flat, horizontal spin. The lift would be upward and would keep it from falling to the ground. This instinct, however, proves disastrous in practice. When thrown this way, the boomerang climbs straight up, pauses, then plummets to a crash landing. One Australian manufacturer prints a warning on the back of his boomerangs: "Never throw up!" This is good advice.

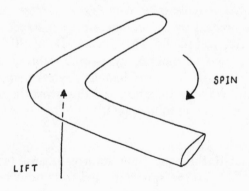

A proper throw leaves the boomerang spinning almost *vertically*. The aerodynamic lifting force is directed largely to the side and is tilted up only slightly. (For convenience, the spinning boomerang will be pictured as a disk, because the arms have a circular movement.)

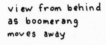

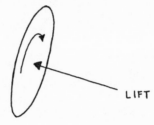

view from behind as boomerang moves away

LIFT

HORIZON

Because returning boomerangs are not very heavy (typically 3½ ounces) the slight upward tilt of the lifting force is sufficient to counteract gravity and prevent an early collision with the ground.

The major part of the lift is directed sideways; you might suspect that this is responsible for the returning behavior. But once again a guess proves misleading. A sideways force alone would pull the boomerang into a diagonal path, but would not make it return. You would merely retrieve it from a different corner of the field. We should note, however, that this force plays an important role. The side force does not *cause* the turn, but it does help the boomerang make a tighter circle by counteracting centrifugal force.

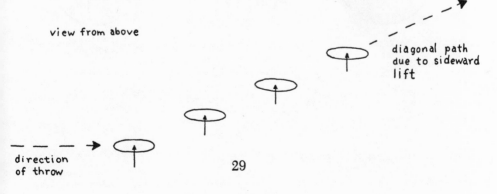

view from above

diagonal path due to sideward lift

direction of throw

29

To return, the boomerang must *turn*. This sounds obvious enough, but it means that some force must push more strongly on the front edge of the boomerang disk than the rear edge. This unbalanced force is the key to the returning flight of the boomerang. Where does the force come from?

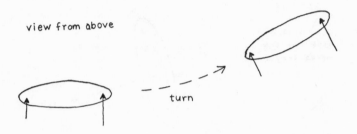

view from above

turn

The turning force originates in the unequal airspeeds of the spinning arms. The boomerang is moving forward as well as rotating. When an arm passes over the top, it is spinning in a forward direction. This forward spin adds to the forward motion of the entire boomerang, producing (for an instant) a very high speed. When the same arm later passes the bottom, its backward motion reduces its speed through the air.

high speed through air

forward motion of boomerang

low speed through air

The boomerang arm, like any wing, will produce more lift when it is passing through the air at a higher speed.

The arms, therefore, generate more lift at the top of the disk than at the bottom. This extra lift at the top, when coupled with gyroscopic precession, can make the boomerang turn.

Precession is a little-known phenomenon which affects all spinning objects. When a force attempts to tilt a spinning object, the object mysteriously responds by tilting in another direction. To be precise, the tilt response will "lag" 90° behind the applied force. A simple example may help.

If you push on a spinning top (below) to make it tilt north, it will respond by tilting east. Reverse the direction of spin and it will tilt west. The response is always 90° away from the applied force in the direction of the spin.

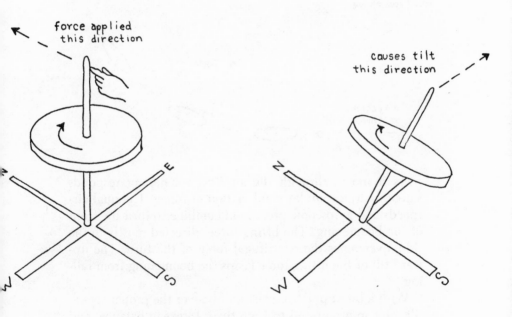

For the boomerang, precession has the following application: the excess lift produced by the greater airspeed of the arm passing the top of the disk will not produce a tilt at the top. Instead, precession will intervene, and the tilt will appear 90° farther around the disk. The front edge of the disk

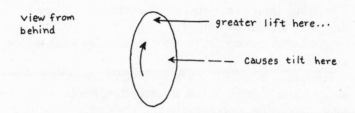

view from
behind

greater lift here...

causes tilt here

will be pushed to the side—exactly what is needed to make
the boomerang turn and return.

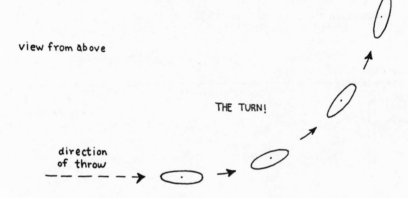

view from above

THE TURN!

direction
of throw

As it moves through the air, the boomerang responds
smoothly to a complex combination of forces. Unequal airspeeds and gyroscopic precession combine to turn the front
of the boomerang. The lifting force, directed mostly to the
side, overcomes the centrifugal force of the turn. The upward tilt of the lifting force keeps the boomerang from falling.

With a bit of practice you can discover the proper speed,
tilt, and spin required to keep these forces in balance, and
can see the boomerang float gently back to your hand.

This wasn't so complex after all, was it?

MAKING ONE'S OWN,
OR MANY HAPPY RETURNS

Constructing a boomerang is quick, easy, and doesn't require many tools, although if your home workshop is well equipped, the job will go more smoothly.

A saw, a rasp, a plane, sandpaper, and decorating materials are all you need, plus plywood for the boomerang blank. Other materials such as hardwood, plastic laminates, fiberglass, and even metal can be used for boomerangs when you feel like experimenting, but plywood is an unbeatable starting material. It's strong, inexpensive, easy to work with, and readily available. If you can find an offcut piece, you might even get it free.

The design of this beginner's boomerang is a simple one and is particularly appropriate for first efforts. If made with reasonable care and attention to the plan, your first boomerang should perform well, making a wide, curving flight back to you and hovering just a bit until it drops to the grass at your feet.

The design is flexible and can be adapted to larger and smaller boomerangs. You can experiment, too, with the angle between the wings. The range can be from 80° to 120°, with a sharper curve yielding a faster turn and a shallower angle giving a more interesting and variable flight.

If you're left-handed, simply reverse the plan so that you construct a mirror image. If in doubt, hold the plan up to a mirror and proceed from the image you see there.

The boomerang should yield months, even years, of service if you can refrain from bouncing it off automobiles, fences, poles, and other unyielding obstacles. Store it pressed flat, away from moisture. If by some misfortune it breaks, don't despair. Just glue it together with white household glue. Depending on the break, you may have to apply a splint for added strength. This support, of course, must be sanded down to cut friction.

After the bonding, you may be surprised to find your boomerang actually flying better than before because of the improved dynamic balance caused by a slight realignment of the wings and a change in weighting from the glue and the splint.

Here's how to make your boomerang:

1/ Obtain some birch plywood 3/8" thick. Plywood 1/4" thick is a reasonable alternative. Ask for aircraft or marine plywood, although any exterior grade will do. The wood you choose should be free of surface blemishes and should be unwarped. An 18" square will yield three or four boomerang blanks.

2/ Make a pattern of stiff cardboard in the shape shown on the plan. Note that if your piece of plywood is slightly warped, the pattern should be marked out on the concave or "dished" side to give the wing tips an upward tilt. This upward tilt won't affect the boomerang's flight, whereas a downward one might make the boomerang dive to the ground during its flight—clearly not what you have in mind.

3/ Cut the boomerang blank with a coping saw, or with another available saw.

4/ To guide you in shaping the boomerang, draw guidelines on the boomerang with a soft pencil. Mark a line all

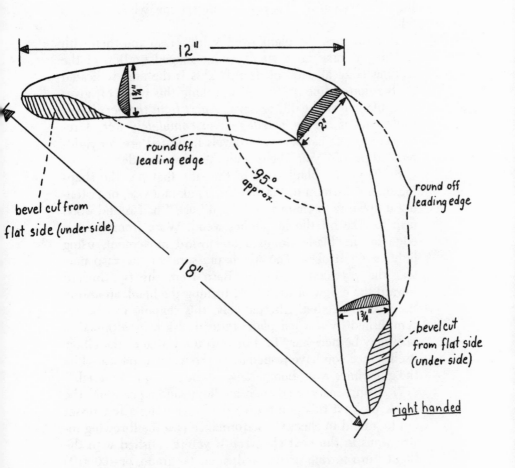

12"

1¾"

round off
leading edge

2"

round off
leading edge

95°
approx.

bevel cut from
flat side (underside)

18"

1¾"

bevel cut
from flat side
(under side)

<u>right</u> <u>handed</u>

end view of wingtip
(exaggerated)

around the upper surface of the blank approximately 1/4" in from the leading edge and 1/2" in from the trailing edge. Consult the plan to determine which edge is which.

5/ Now turn the blank over. With a rasp and then with sandpaper, take off a small wedge-shaped portion of the leading edge at each blade tip. This is the area indicated by the dotted line on the plan. Taking this wood off gives each blade a slight tilt, or bevel. *Apart from the bevels, the underside of the wing will remain completely flat.* A reminder to left-handers: the bevels indicated are for right-handed people; yours belong on the opposite sides.

6/ Turn the blank over to the side that has the shaping lines drawn on it. Placing the blank in a vise, or fastening it down with clamps, use a 3/4" or 1" half-round wood rasp to take off the remaining wood. Work from the top edge of the blade tip in a downward movement, using light, even strokes. Too much pressure on the rasp may tear the plywood laminates. Rasp from the tips inward toward the elbow of the blank, turning the blank around in the vise as needed. Alternatively, this shaping can be accomplished by a wood plane instead of a rasp, although a rasp may be necessary to deal with the inside of the elbow itself. Once you have rasped away the wood as indicated by the guidelines, your boomerang will be nearly completed.

7/ Using coarse and then medium sandpaper, sand the blank well. At this point, give the boomerang a few tosses out in a field to check its performance (see the throwing instructions in the next chapter). If you're satisfied with the flight, turn to fine grade sandpaper (00 grade, or 400 grit) to finish off the job. A warning: don't thin the blades down too far or they'll nick when they hit the ground. The tips, particularly, should be left a little blunt because they take the most impact.

8/ You're ready to decorate your boomerang now. If you want a handsome boomerang, finish it off with Johnson's floor wax. Brown shoe polish works well, too. Enamel paint can also be used, with stripes or other decorations added to make your handiwork eye-catching. The boomerang can also be shellacked, varnished, or stained. Another satisfactory procedure is to draw designs on the raw wood with a ball-point pen and then decorate inside the drawn designs with a felt-tip marker. Spraying over this with polyurethane protects your artwork and gives the boomerang a pleasing high-gloss finish. Note that all these modes of decorating serve to waterproof the boomerang as well, a useful step.

So now you've got a boomerang, and the action switches from indoors to outdoors.

THROWER AS TARGET

If you're not critically uncoordinated, you can throw a boomerang so that it will return to you. You can catch the boomerang, too. *The New York Times* sports columnist Red Smith made a perfect first throw; with his second effort, he was able to catch his returning boomerang. I've never seen anyone catch the thing on the very first try, but Henry Tenenbaum, a commentator for Washington's WTOP-TV, almost did. His boomerang came neatly back into his hands; unnerved, he juggled the spinning object and dropped it.

The point is, it's easy. If you can throw a baseball decently, you can throw a boomerang.

Where?

On a large, grassy, empty field. Something about the size of a baseball field. Then if your boomerang goes awry because of bad aim, or is caught by a sudden breeze, you can't do any damage. When you get good and know your boomerang, you can throw in smaller spaces for admiring throngs. At the beginning, though, give yourself elbow room.

Remember that once the boomerang leaves your hand, it may fly a course a bit different from the one you envisioned. And arguments with owners of dented autos, broken windows, and sobbing children are preferably avoided. At the start, especially, throw with caution.

The way to keep control is to throw only when there is little or no wind. Well-made, light boomerangs perform perfectly well with no wind at all and are in fact most accurate in a dead calm.

A light breeze is fine to throw in, but if the wind is blowing at much more than five to seven miles an hour, things quickly become hopeless. The boomerang gets blown back to you, but then just keeps sailing past you, and you have a long walk to retrieve it. If there's a strong wind, go fly a kite.

Assuming that you have found a clear field and a still day, grip your boomerang between the thumb and first and second fingers of your hand, with the point projecting away from you, sickle-style. The V of the boomerang points over the shoulder. The round side is toward you, the flat side facing away. Be sure to overlap the end of the boomerang with your index finger; that's the finger that trips it upon release and gives it great spin.

Hold it vertically (1) or tilted to the right a bit (/). Never hold it horizontally (—). These instructions, by the way, are for right-handed throwers. Lefties must reverse the directions as well as use a left-handed boomerang, the mirror image of a right-handed one.

Hold the boomerang close to its end in a firm grip. Don't hold it too tightly. This will curb the wrist and finger action that imparts the necessary spin. And spin is what keeps the thing airborne.

Stance is also important. Stand with your feet together, and then as you prepare to fire away, take a step forward with your left leg. (Take a step forward with your right leg if you are left-handed.) This looks athletic, keeps you from falling over, and accentuates body swing to give force to the throw.

Finally, aim the boomerang level with the horizon, or at treetops in the distance.

After a couple of practices without releasing the boomerang, you're ready. Think of cracking a whip; upon release, you'll jerk your wrist back sharply. Now cock your arm back, take a step, and let the boomerang fly. It should whirl out, curve to the left, climb a bit, come curving back to you, and land close by. If the thing has died out a bit toward the end, you probably haven't hurled it with enough zip. Try again.

The average thrower, incidentally, launches a boomerang at about sixty miles an hour and ten revolutions per second. At this speed, the boomerang should make a faint whirring sound; no sound means you're probably not throwing hard enough.

To review, throw vertically or nearly so, aim at the horizon for a flat flight, and snap your wrist on release.

Although it's best to throw in a dead calm, such a condition is rare. Ordinarily you'll have some wind to contend with. You can judge its direction and force by dropping a few pieces of grass. It helps to observe the direction in which tree leaves are blowing. A thread held in the hand is useful.

When launching, throw to the right of the wind (left-handed people should face to the left). Make the boomerang fight the breeze. If it lands in front of you, aim farther into the wind. If it lands in back of you, which is most likely, aim more to the right. Picture a clock and launch toward three o'clock. If the boomerang hits in back of you, aim toward four o'clock.

In practice, accounting for the breeze quickly becomes a habit. But at first, pay strict attention. Despite instructions, many people, especially youngsters, insist on launching boomerangs sidearm, in what they consider to be appropriate Frisbee manner. Tossed in this manner, the boomerang climbs high, stalls, and comes hurtling back the way it went up, only to crash hard on the ground. Do this sidearm throw once too often, and you'll have two pieces of boomerang. *Throw vertically.*

With a good boomerang and a bit of finesse in the throwing, you'll quickly learn to bring the boomerang back with precision. Many athletically inclined people can throw almost perfectly within five minutes. If thrown hard enough and with enough spin, the boomerang will not only come back but fly one or two or even three small circles around you before lightly dropping to the grass. Instead of circles, sometimes it flies in the shape of a figure S.

You'll now want to test your skill in catching the boomerang in midair as it drops down in its slow hover. Watch its descent, get into position, and clap the boomerang between your outstretched palms, keeping fingers well away. Make a boomerang sandwich.

If you've got the boomerang performing well and coming down in a hover, catching is much easier than it sounds. Witness one Texan's record claim of 388 consecutive catches. Great skill was involved, but what a boring thing to have done!

The trick to catching a boomerang is in the timing; if its hover is not perfectly flat, the judging of the boomerang's pendulum swoops at the end of its flight is of critical importance. If you want to show off to your friends, you'll want to learn to catch. Besides—and this is really the point —catching gives the flight that ultimate poetic perfection. Your airborne flying stick returns to you obediently and lands in your hands without ever having touched the ground. It's flight as man dreams of it.

With boomerangs, things are rarely simple. Witness the issue of the grip. I have just advised you to hold the boomerang sickle-style, with the vee of the boomerang facing backward. This is the classic aboriginal technique. However, you can just as well hold the boomerang with one end facing over your shoulder (round side toward you, though, as in the aboriginal mode); in fact, you may find that you get a smoother launch this way. For years, I've been a dev-

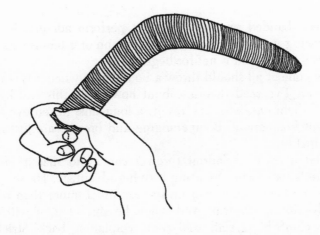

otee of the aboriginal grip, and I've now switched to the point-over-shoulder style. The release is smoother, and I feel that I put more zip in the launch.

Try the two techniques for yourself and decide.

If you've made a boomerang from the plan given in the preceding chapter, some words on flight testing are in order.

Does the boomerang dive down about halfway around? If so, the problem may be in the throw. Try tilting the boomerang to the right a bit, and be sure to give it plenty of spin and forward thrust. If the boomerang still dives into the grass, it may have too little lift. In this case, cut the bevels deeper in the wing tips.

Does the boomerang climb too high? If so, make sure you are launching vertically. If soaring continues, you may have to curb the boomerang's lift. Reduce the width of the arm somewhat. Or try putting tape on the wing tips and at the center to add some weight.

Does your boomerang lose spin rapidly? If so, it may not be adequately finished. Rough surfaces create drag. Try sandpapering the boomerang so it feels really smooth. In sanding, give particular attention to edges and tips.

Want to try a splashy effect? A right-handed person can take a leftie boomerang, or a left-handed thrower can take a right-handed one, and make it perform adequately by throwing it across his face in simulation of a tennis smash. This is showy and is not for beginners.

No one at all should throw a boomerang when it is really breezy. I've read theories about how to do this and have tried them out, with one result: a long hike to retrieve the errant boomerang. Boomeranging and breezes are just not compatible.

But a really maladroit thrower can avoid shame when there is some wind by using it to his advantage. He simply tilts the boomerang over on its side much more than normal—almost sidearm. And when he throws it, it will go out, climb high, stall, and come volplaning back. Strictly speaking, it's not a boomerang throw; if tried by someone with a strong arm who puts a lot of speed and spin into the delivery, it creates a dangerous missile. But for the person who can barely launch a boomerang to begin with (and there are some of these, alas), such a delivery is a last resort. This is an ideal way to avoid disgrace.

I'm not exactly a maladroit thrower, but I've sometimes thought I was. Once, throwing before a crowd of children at a private school in Alexandria, Virginia, I found that my best efforts at gauging the wind coupled with my finest launches failed to produce returns. The site was a hilltop field from which radiated lanes of trees. I faced a second direction. Then a third and a fourth. Still there were no returns. The boomerang whirled around busily, but it wouldn't come back, or even come close. I was acutely embarrassed by that time because the instructor had given me a rather fulsome introduction. "Impossible wind conditions," I explained. It was not too convincing, because I wasn't sure of the problem myself.

After a second such episode, I understand better what went wrong. Throwing for a television film team on the National Mall in Washington, I positioned the cameraman so he could record the catch. But my repeated throws failed to produce returns. It was my favorite boomerang, and I was throwing well. The cameraman smirked at the audio man. The commentator smiled at both of them. Shamed and rather desperate, I looked around and saw things were quite normal, except that some distance away was a line of tourist buses, parked side by side and quite empty of people. Because it was a hot day, their engines were idling; I realized that these idling engines would create hot exhausts and disturbed air. But weren't we far enough away to escape any possible effects? I took our group a hundred yards away, not without some grumbling on the part of the cameraman. I let the boomerang fly. Around the boomerang went, past me, making a small circle overhead, a second circle, and descending into my waiting hands. I hadn't taken more than a step or two. There were smiles all around. And we proceeded with a half hour of filming.

The two incidents taught me about the complexity of air currents. Though invisible, they're a factor to be reckoned with in boomerang throwing. If things aren't going smoothly for you, and if you seem to be throwing well, stop and examine the situation. Maybe a move to another site is necessary.

One illustrious boomerang thrower was Vice-President Henry Wallace, who got his morning exercise by tossing around returners. A problem was that as a noteworthy politician he drew journalistic coverage and, as I made clear earlier, having too many people around when one is throwing boomerangs can lead to trouble.

Byron "Beano" Rollins, an Associated Press photographer in Washington, D.C., recently recalled for me an incident in West Potomac Park that gained both him and Wallace some unwanted notoriety. Beano recalls that it occurred when Wallace was Secretary of Agriculture, before 1941.

Wallace and Supreme Court Justice William Jackson were throwing boomerangs in order to get some exercise. Beano, then working for Times Wide World Photos, was taking pictures of the two of them. Wallace launched a boomerang that swung around toward Rollins. "Look out, Beano!" someone shouted. He looked up from the viewfinder. Zap! The boomerang bounced off his head. His fellow journalists laughed, while Wallace hurried up to inspect the damage. "It wasn't that serious, except that it scraped the top of my head off," recalls Beano. A hospital bandaged him up, and the following day one Washington newspaper carried a headline that read: "Who Beaned Beano?"

"I didn't have a headache out of it, just a little embarrassment," says Beano now. "How good a thrower was Wallace?" he is asked. "He threw well enough to hit me," is his response.

This leaves Wallace's prowess as a boomerang-thrower somewhat up in the air. What is not to be doubted is the expertise of many throwers around the world. Some of the records and feats compiled over the years are remarkable. But in considering them in the next pages, one should not forget a dictum current in Australian boomerang throwing circles: Skillful liars far outnumber skillful boomerang throwers.

BAREFOOT CATCHING
AND OTHER FEATS

"In 1955," writes Octave Levenspiel of Oregon State University, "while teaching at Bucknell University, idiocy prompted me to see how many times I could throw and catch a boomerang successfully. Result: Fifty-nine catches within a one-hour period. Feeling that I should be compensated somehow for my sore arm, I then claimed the Eastern U.S. title (my natural modesty limited my claim to the East). The school paper reported it and a few years later a national magazine repeated this 'news' in its miscellany section, next to the interesting tidbit that the U.S. imported 7,643,432 corks from Portugal in the first three months of 1923 . . . or some such thing. Sad to say, no one has challenged me since then."

Now that's the right approach. Modern-day boomerang throwing is distinguished by a fun-and-games amateurishness, and the whole business of record-keeping should be kept lighthearted.

After all, ten thousand—or perhaps one hundred thousand—years of good throws by aborigines have gone unrecorded. Stone Age man didn't bother marking down longest throws or best catches. Western man, however, likes competition and scoring and all the paraphernalia that goes with record-keeping. So records are being kept now—by me.

No one else was keeping track. And through correspondence, I came to know boomerang fanatics all over the world. We tend to seek one another out, and we're enthusiastic letter writers. Several years ago, I began to keep a file on the record claims of amateurs and semi-professionals around the world. The authors of the *Guinness Book of World Records* heard about this and wrote for help in its listing, which I was pleased to give.

My own file of records circulated worldwide, causing boomerang throwers to try to break the ones listed and invent new ones. Claims proliferated, some of which are rather surprising.

I'm not certifying any of these records. Many are unsubstantiated. Anyway, I throw best when nobody is around, and I assume most other people do, too. But it's worthwhile listing these feats as an indication of what can actually be done with a boomerang. They also show the direction the sport might take if it becomes popular and well-organized, as it is beginning to be in Australia.

Here, then, are some of the accomplishments:

John McMahon, of San Padre Island, Texas, says he has caught 388 boomerangs in a row. This breaks his old mark of 172, which broke a previous record of 157. McMahon simultaneously throws three boomerangs with his right hand and one with his left hand, and then he catches all four when they come back to him. He once caught 37 boomerangs in a row behind his back. A beach regular, McMahon makes boomerangs and lays them out on the sand; he is willing to peddle his wares to passersby and throw in a free lesson besides. It's not a bad living, he reports.

The late Frank Donnellan (not killed by a boomerang, I'm happy to report) caught boomerangs blindfolded before crowds in theaters, judging the position of the device

48

by the whirring sound it made. Donnellan, a Sydney printer, was also a brave man. He would mount a big apple on his head, launch a boomerang, and on its return let the device knock the apple off his head. This William Tell-like feat was once performed on the stage of the Tivoli Theater in Sydney.

Herb Smith, of Sussex, England, gets the prize for quantity tossing. Launching boomerangs one at a time as fast as he could, Smith managed to put eleven into the air before the first one came down. The fly-past of boomerangs must have been a beautiful picture. Joe Timbery, the noted aboriginal thrower from Sydney, got ten in the air at one time during a performance at Wagga Wagga for Queen Elizabeth II's 1954 visit to Australia. (He can also catch a boomerang with his bare feet.) Colonel John Gerrish, of Portland, Oregon, equalled the ten-in-the-air-feat on the "You Asked For It" television show in New York in 1955.

When he visited the United States in 1969, Dutch physicist Felix Hess threw a boomerang completely around the Washington Monument. Dimensions at the base are 55½-by-55½-feet.

Dennis Maxwell, of Dinley, Australia, has made thirty-six one-handed catches in a row. The trick here is to grab for the imaginary spot in the air around which the boomerang is spinning without taking a rap on the knuckles. This is not for beginners.

Comedian Fred Stone had an unusual act. He'd strap a tin can on top of his head and then launch a six-armed boomerang bolted at the center over the audience in a theater. When the boomerang whirled back, he would catch the bolt in his can. The boomerang would continue to spin fast, giving Stone the look of a Martian.

Robert Boys, of Merriam, Kansas, once made eleven catches in a row without moving his feet an inch.

Cabinetmaker Howard Baker, of Balby, England, attained esthetic perfection one day. He simultaneously tossed one boomerang right-handed and one left-handed, and then had them land exactly between his feet, one on top of the other.

In a distance competition for small boomerangs, Joe Lewry, of Bowna, New South Wales, threw a midget boomerang measuring approximately five inches more than twenty-five yards outward and brought it back to the small throwing circle from which he launched it.

I. S. "Bluey" Williams, of Melbourne, made ten catches in an eight yard circle in four minutes and eighteen seconds. Try this competition sometime when you need exercise.

The foregoing gives you an idea of how sporty boomerang-throwing can be.

Now we come to the serious record—distance. It's important because it's a supreme test. To be able to throw a boomerang almost out of sight and bring it back for the catch commands the attention of absolutely everyone.

Frank Donnellan, the Australian, claimed two world's record distance throws—160 yards out and back, and 140 yards out and back with a catch. He dated them May 4, 1934, at Centennial Park, Sydney. Witnesses were reportedly on hand. I've been unable to obtain any independent substantiation of his claims, however, such as a newspaper account. This is magnificent throwing. After all, 160 yards is more than a football field and a half in length.

Donnellan, who died in 1969 at the age of 70, had learned about boomerangs as a child from aborigines at Botany Bay and gave demonstrations for much of his life. Only five feet four inches tall, he is described as having been strong and sprightly, and photographs bear this out. As a young man, he had been a bantamweight boxer.

According to Mrs. Stephen Silady (Pauline Pawlow, the Australian poet), Donnellan threw at agricultural fairs and in theaters, made a demonstration tour of New Zealand, and once journeyed to England to appear on television. He is buried in North Ryde, not far from Chatswood, New South Wales. Upon his death people on his street honored his memory by placing a six-foot boomerang of flowers on his grave.

Donnellan in his promotional literature billed himself as the "holder of all records," but contemporary Australian boomerang-throwers dispute his claims, although they concede he was a mighty thrower. The long-distance boomerangs Donnellan made and sold are still around and are being hurled by some of the strong young throwers who compete in tournaments today. They are not producing the distance Donnellan claimed to have achieved. Not close to it, I'm told. Perhaps the problem is in Donnellan's measuring. I'll leave the argument to the Australians.

I do wish, however, to pay honor to a man who kept the sport going in the thirties and forties, when there was very little interest in it, and who was a pioneer in designing and manufacturing high-performance boomerangs. One of them, a small plastic model, is still manufactured by Stephen Silady and sold around the world. Silady designed the mold from which the mass-produced boomerang is made. It's a first-rate performer, but it's hard for the novice to throw well. It takes a lot of snap in the toss.

Donnellan was a tireless evangelist of the boomerang and once gave a demonstration at a school. As was his custom, he left a few boomerangs behind. The headmaster was unenthusiastic. He told Donnellan the students had more than enough sports to occupy them, including tennis, cricket, and boating. Some days later, Donnellan visited the school again and noticed a broken window. A student told him the headmaster had done it—with a boomerang.

As far as a distance record is concerned, the claim made by Herb Smith cannot be ignored. He is a penal officer in the south of England and a maker of extraordinarily finely crafted boomerangs. Smith's record throw is 108 yards, one foot, four inches. Precise? Yes. Smith made elaborate preparations to measure his throws accurately.

His account of the record throw is interesting and so well documented it's worth reproducing, in part:

"Shortly after making my first boomerang, I became interested in throwing for long distance. . . . I began to experiment with weight-balancing and ballasting, as the plywood I was using (good birch ply, one-quarter, three-eighths, and one-half inch thick) was, in my opinion, too light in weight. My first method of weighting was to strap small disks of lead to the blades in various positions, and I eventually found that a weight of approximately three-quarters of an ounce on each blade tip (for a boomerang weighing six ounces) increased the distance three times without affecting its flight path and return accuracy.

"Of course, it was necessary to throw with much more force to get the boomerang to return successfully and quite often the boomerang would pitch downward on its initial turn and smash into the ground. For this type of weighted boomerang, a wind of approximately five to seven miles per hour is ideal. Anything stronger, and the outward distance is reduced by as much as ten per cent and the thing lands some sixty yards behind the throwing line, sometimes even more.

"After the initial trial-and-error with the weight strapped to the boomerang, I make suitably shaped lead or metal plugs and insert these into holes drilled through the blade.

"I have thrown this type of boomerang over a hundred and twenty yards *unofficially* and had a complete return back to the throwing mark. . . .

"On June 17, 1972, I made a measured throw of a hundred eight yards, one foot, four inches.

"Having informed the local press of my intention to make an officially witnessed throw of a hundred yards or more, I made arrangements with the authorities of the Littlehampton Sports Club to use the cricket pitch for a series of throws. Six volunteers agreed to act as stewards and the head groundsman of the sports club agreed to do the measuring. I took with me two fiberglass boomerangs and one of birch ply. The day was sunny and warm with a gusty wind of approximately eighteen to twenty miles per hour. I had two pegs on the throwing line placed in the ground seven feet apart with a steward standing a few feet either side of the pegs to make certain I didn't step over the line when throwing and also to witness the boomerang's complete return back over the line.

"The other four stewards were standing at a distance beyond ninety yards a few feet apart from each other. They each had a bundle of wooden pegs, and, as I threw, they placed a peg in the ground in front of them as the boomerang circled behind them. I made a series of throws with the fiberglass boomerangs, all over ninety yards and back. The best throws were ninety-three, ninety-seven and a half and a hundred three and a half yards. I then made a few throws with the birch ply boomerang, reaching a distance of a hundred eight yards, one foot, four inches.

"To make an accurate measurement, the groundsman used a nylon line which he stretched from each distance peg to the center of my two throwing pegs. Then, using a steel measuring tape a hundred feet long, he measured along the nylon line, pegging the ground every hundred feet. The throws were witnessed by some twenty-odd spectators, including several press photographers and members of the sports club."

A convincing account. And bravo to Smith for introducing some careful documentation into a sport in which it has been noticeably lacking.

Four other contemporary throwers are claiming distance throws with returns in the one-hundred-yard range. They are Silady, Donnellan's disciple; the Burwell brothers, Bob and Jack, of Ormeau, Queensland; and Jeff Lewry, of Bowna, New South Wales.

Winner of the Australian championship, Lewry always has to throw at his best to top his lovely and strong-armed blonde daughter, Carol. Once, on tour in New Zealand, he was warming up for a demonstration when he made a heave that circled well behind a range steward standing eighty-five measured yards away from him. The boomerang returned with precision. Lewry made just a single step to the side to grab it with one hand against his thigh.

For sheer expertise, Australian nightclub performer Bevan Rayner tops everyone. He's a professional who makes a living by throwing boomerangs, and his achievements reflect this. This is the act he's been doing in English nightclubs over the past few years:

He starts the show as if he were doing a balancing, juggling act, using a sword. He then removes his coat and hangs it carefully on a coat hanger, which he entrusts to a mechanical kangaroo. A built-in, delayed-action device causes the kangaroo to turn and knock the coat and hanger to the floor after Rayner turns his back. This keeps on happening through the act. "There is always someone in the audience who will laugh," he says.

Eventually he becomes exasperated and hurls the coat hanger at the kangaroo. But the coat hanger is actually a light-weight boomerang (Rayner has several with various turning circles for different clubs), and it flies around and back, knocking him down. This introduces the unusual part of the act.

Rayner throws and catches a boomerang several times, and when conditions are ideal, he tosses one which appears to fall short, almost touching the floor about eight feet away from him, but then rising to be caught again at shoulder height. He then keeps two boomerangs in the air by throwing the second before catching the first. He says he has kept three or even four going when practicing, but not when working in front of an audience.

Rayner throws two together (one having a slightly larger turning circle), throws one left-handed, then tosses some oddly shaped boomerangs. One looks like a large pair of scissors—a very light spring keeps it in the wide-open position. He also has a three-armed boomerang with lights on the tips to throw during a blackout.

He has a pair of three-armed boomerangs, one left-handed and the other right-handed, that he starts throwing, and then he keeps them flying. By rotating himself half a turn after each throw, he keeps one in the air in front of him and one in the air behind him, giving a pleasing pattern. By rotating himself a little more or a little less than a half turn each time, the whole pattern rotates.

Rayner also has a three-armed boomerang that makes two circles before returning, or, it might be said, returns twice from one throw. Finally, he hurls a three-armed boomerang with a hole in the center and catches it on a stiletto held in his mouth. Needless to say, the mechanical kangaroo also throws a boomerang.

It sounds like an entertaining act.

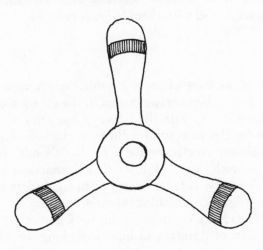

With the exception of Joe Timbery, not one of the foregoing throwers mentioned is an aborigine. Why not? Surely
aborigines in Australia over the millennia performed feats
the equal of many of those listed, even though their boomerangs might have been made of relatively inefficient
wood; wood doesn't begin to compare with, say, nylon re-
inforced with fiberglass as a material for making high performance boomerangs.

We can do no more than speculate about the aborigines.
Combing the very extensive literature of the past two centuries of white observation yields little information. Reports
of aboriginal feats are imprecise; distances can only be estimated. There are obvious wild exaggerations. Throws of
150 yards outward, seemingly a favorite distance, are common; boomerangs reportedly climb to 150 feet in the air;
they apparently circle almost endlessly. They stop to hover
in the distance before coming back in a rush to the
thrower.

What these accounts convey is exceptional skill on the
part of some native throwers, but they give nothing very
precise as far as measurements are concerned. Without reli-
able eyewitness reports, we have only one piece of evidence from the eighteenth- and nineteenth-century past to
work with: the old boomerangs, themselves preserved in
collections. Studies of these devices will yield some insights, but we'll never be certain what Herculean feats
were accomplished with them in years gone by.

One record we haven't probed is duration. A person guess-
ing how long a boomerang stayed in the air on a calm day
will often come up with the figure of one minute. This appears to be the case until a flight is clocked. The actual
time is almost exactly twelve seconds. It's odd, but true.
Test it yourself. In a high wind, a boomerang performs
quite differently. It takes energy from the breeze and may
fly a great distance, spinning nonstop.

Felix Hess has a computer at his beck and call, and I put
the question of duration to him. How long would a boo-

merang stay up if launched from an aerial balloon, for instance?

Hess projected a modest launch from ninety meters and sent me the printout from the computer. In this simulated flight, the boomerang goes around, makes a small circle, and drops down to the launch point. Because there is no one to catch it and because there isn't ground for it to hit, the boomerang falls and falls and then begins to open up a circle until it achieves approximately the orbit it had originally. Taking energy from gravity, it spins and spins in a free fall that resembles the autumnal plunge of a maple leaf.

From this, one deduces that a boomerang, if launched from a balloon at ten thousand feet, would take a long time to come down; it might even rise now and then if caught in a thermal. You might hit an unsuspecting person up to twenty miles away.

"Lurk" is an Australian slang word whose definition is evident. A lurk is something cleverly underhanded. Australians report that lurks are occurring in boomerang throwing these days.

For instance, tie a piece of thin, strong cord between the wing tips. It helps in catching the boomerang. In distance throwing on a breezy day, use a windbreak, such as a line of trees or a railroad embankment. The boomerang goes out a long way in the lee, then rises up to be met by the strong wind and gets blown back to the point of dispatch.

Hoping to add boomeranging to the Olympics, partisans in Australia now talk about restricting boomerang records to those set in those tournaments where the wind is below a given velocity. Track and field competition scores, they point out, are disallowed if the wind is too helpful.

My feeling is that such restrictions are not a bad idea for the future, but they do threaten to make the sport too serious. I'm all for the national Frisbee tournament mentality. As its prize, the championship team gets to drink beer

out of a rusty old tomato can. Why try to turn boomeranging into pro football?

Lorin Hawes, the Mudgeeraba craftsman, gets the last
word. He feels boomerang feats are mainly good for the
ego. Dr. Hawes likes to throw two boomerangs at once and
catch them both when they return. He's done it a number
of times, and he says that it adds variety to life. But, he
confesses, "It is terribly aggravating if there is nobody
there to witness your having done it."

GAMES THE
GUNDAWARRA* PLAY

Now you can make and throw boomerangs, and what you want is some competition. After all, it's the American way. Take a nice, solitary, peaceful pastime and add hostility and aggression to it. This is called a game.

Peter Ruhf, of Berkeley, California, has invented a boomerang competition called "Out Back" that is simplicity itself. You need boomerangs, a clear field, a calm day, and a few handkerchiefs or shirts, or whatever rags you may have lying around.

Make a circle by placing your markers around an imaginary circumference. The circle should be approximately fifteen feet in diameter (its dimensions can be changed during the throwing, depending on how well the scoring is going). Mark the center of the circle with something that won't be ruined by being stepped on and ground into the

*An aboriginal word for white men who play with boomerangs.

grass—Peter Ruhf used his fiancee's jacket the first time he organized a competition, and there were repercussions.

Three to six contestants is a reasonable number of players to start with. Decide on the throwing order by volunteering, if the people are reasonable, or drawing numbers out of a hat if they aren't. Everyone gets one free throw to test the wind.

You can launch the boomerang from any place you want. The trick is to make sure it concludes its flight right in the center of the circle. If the thrower has his foot on the center point when he makes his catch, he gets ten points. If he catches it with his foot anywhere inside the circle, he gets seven points. If he manages to catch it outside the circle, he gets five. If he touches but drops the returning boomerang while his foot is on the center point, he scores three; if he's inside the circle, two; and outside the circle, one. Leaps to catch or touch are okay—where you land determines what you get.

When you see the game in progress, you'll get the idea: throw, get to the center of the circle, plant your toe on it, and then make the big stretch for the returning boomerang. No easy grabs against the chest; the thrower must gamble with dangerous catches, which causes a lot of tension. This produces misses at key moments, especially since heckling is allowed, not to say encouraged.

The winner is the thrower who has accumulated the highest score in two of three rounds of five throws each, or he can be the person with the most points for all the rounds taken together. Don't decide in advance; like all flexible rules, this can be heatedly argued after the game. And don't appoint a judge, either; let the contestants do the judging. Things are more dramatic that way.

This delightful game was first played on a gray Thanksgiving Day at the Bucks County, Pennsylvania, home of writers George and Helen Papashvily. All the players were siblings or otherwise related, which made them competitive; they were good throwers; and they had perfect throwing conditions. The competition was distinctly intense, even brutal. The scores reflected this—out of fifty possible points in one round, the winner scored in the forties and five

60

other contestants in the thirties. Anyone who wasn't catching on the center point almost all the time was disgraced. That's how accurate boomerang throwing can get.

Another game is "The Impromptu." Even beginners can win in this simple-minded contest. Here are the rules: each person gets just one throw. He is not allowed to touch his returning boomerang. The winner is the thrower who takes the fewest steps to get from his throwing point to the spot on the ground where his boomerang hits. Height is an advantage here, as giant steps and leaps are permitted.

It doesn't take much ingenuity to think up other competitions. Balloon busting is one. Consecutive catching is another—drop a boomerang, and you're out of the contest. For experts, juggling is sporty: using two boomerangs, try to keep one flying at all times as you catch and throw, catch and throw, catch and throw.

A competition testing how many catches can be made in a given period of time—two minutes, for instance—is fun for the spectators and hard work for the competitors. Launching three boomerangs at once or firing them in rapid succession is fine. The trick, of course, is in the catching when they all return. (It's pretty easy to get beaned with one's own boomerang when doing this sort of thing— the boomerang equivalent of getting one's own back.)

The Mudgeeraba Creek Emu Riding and Boomerang Throwing Association, of Mudgeeraba, Queensland, has produced competition rules bearing the unmistakable stamp of Dr. Lorin Hawes, the master carver of Mudgeeraba. Possessor of not one but two doctoral degrees, he is able to append to his name "B.Sc., Ph.D., etc." The "etc." is pure Hawes. Formerly a maker of atomic bombs at Los Alamos, New Mexico, this American expatriate has become a boomerang-maker on a bushland farm near the Gold Coast of Queensland. (There must be a moral in this.)

For outdoor testing of his creations, he has constructed a circular, topless structure which he has dubbed, obviously, a boomerangery.

THE BOOMERANGERY

Mudgeeraba Creek rules test the usual skills—throwing for distance, consecutive catching, accuracy, juggling. A fifth competition is one I'd like to see myself—short-distance throwing. Under the rules, competitors advance toward a wall firing boomerangs in turn. If his boomerang hits, the thrower is out. Finally, one person is left who hasn't struck the wall with his boomerang. He's the winner.

Boomerang tournaments are easy to organize. Dr. Edward F. Blick, an aerospace professor at the University of Oklahoma, engineered a challenge match between five of his students and a team of aerospace students from Oklahoma State University. The thing was billed as the "world's first intercollegiate boomerang throwing contest." Boomerangs were renamed Soonerangs. At the epic event, one student set a world's air-and-water-distance-record for the sport. "The boomerang," reported Dr. Blick, "landed in a creek and washed four blocks away before we could retrieve it."

Among the awards were hamburger dinners at the Boomerang Restaurant in the city of Norman, Oklahoma. Incidentally, Oklahoma University lost.

The Smithsonian's annual boomerang tournament has become a fixture of Washington's spring season, and it draws an increasing number of competitors and bemused spectators each year. For the first few years, the competition was open only to people who had taken the boomerang-making workshop, but throwers from earlier years wanted to compete, and soon we opened it up to everybody. Now the annual throw-in draws folks from all across the country.

As the contest has grown, so has the prize list, so much so that we're hard put to invent enough categories. Our favorite is the "Youngest Illegal Competitor Award," won one year by a seven-year-old who looked five; the minimum entry age is eight. Among the other awards are the "General Douglas MacArthur 'I Shall Return Award,' " the "I-Made-It Myself Prettiest Boomerang Award," and the annual "Polly Ravenscroft Birthday Award." Polly's birthday happened to coincide with the tournament date one year, and she has contributed a prize to the competition ever since. In 1974 it was a home-baked chocolate cake that a *Sports Illustrated* reporter described as being either in the shape of Australia or of a kangaroo—it was hard to decide which.

In a year that a vice-president of the United States was railing at the American press, one pretty female contestant managed to hit a news photographer who insisted on standing directly in her line of fire, urging her to throw her boomerang. When she did throw it, she struck him. We awarded her the Spiro Agnew Memorial Award.

Added attractions are starting to arrive. In 1975, QANTAS brought in its six-foot koala bear—really a suit worn by a man. Every child in the park came tearing up to see the beast with the big ears and fat stomach. Up close, the smallest children backed off after they saw the claws on its paws.

In 1976, our competition became international, with Herb Smith coming in from Sussex and Morris Maxwell coming in from Melbourne. Seventy-two people competed and many hundreds attended, some of whom were drawn from the other all-American sports being played that day on the Mall—rugby on one side and cricket on the other. Among the spectators was writer J. Timberlake Gibson, who termed the competition the next best thing to Washington's singing dog contest.

With the wind down, the throwing was so accurate that we had to devise an expedient to settle the consecutive-catching competition, when two teenaged throwers, Bill Brogan and Joe Dougherty, of McLean, Virginia, threatened to keep the event going all afternoon. We got a winner by invoking a "suicide" rule: they threw simultaneously, and each had to dodge the other while trying to catch his own boomerang. Brogan finally won on the twentieth toss.

The tournament now tests accuracy of return and ability to catch, throwing to the peg (the closest to a marker at the launch site wins), and consecutive catching. We may add other events such as balloon busting, distance throwing, and juggling; seeing who can make the most catches within two minutes is another alternative.

Each year the competition becomes more impressive. As in the case of Bill Brogan, the major winners tend to be iron-nerved teenagers who've learned about boomerangs at the annual Smithsonian workshops and have been practicing ever since in their suburban schoolyards. Among the adults, a young lawyer from Pennsylvania, Larry Fox, amazes everyone each year with his lithe leaps; and Eric Darnell, a young, bearded carpenter from Vermont, who lives in a chicken coop, pleases everyone during the preliminary demonstrations—he throws two boomerangs simultaneously and brings them both back for the catch.

We work to keep the atmosphere casual; the deadly serious competitiveness that ruins some sports is not for us. Along this line, we instantly adopted a rule used by the Mudgeeraba Creek Emu Riding and Boomerang Throwing Association: "Decisions of the judges will be final unless shouted down by a really overwhelming majority of the crowd present. Abusive and obscene language may not be used by contestants when addressing members of the judging panel, or, conversely, by members of the judging panel when addressing contestants (unless struck by a boomerang)."

That sets the right tone.

If you're organizing your own small tournament, you'll find, as we did, that businessmen are quite happy to donate nice prizes in return for a little publicity. If you want media coverage and spectators, be sure to let newspapers and radio and television stations know about your tournament in advance. But be aware that boomerang-throwing attracts publicity, and television crews can take over your contest as they interview people, film the action, and stage throwing sessions of their own on the fringe of the crowd.

All fooling aside, you should have one person in charge of the tournament, and he should keep things under control. Don't allow big, heavy boomerangs in the competition. Have a warm-up area with someone in charge, and don't permit people to go off on their own and throw anywhere they please. Restrict throwing to the warm-up area and the competition circle. A knowledgeable official should be in charge of the actual competition ring. Keep spectators in one big group, and position them away from the line of fire. If the day is really windy, and boomerangs will not be under good control, postpone the tournament.

Now for the rules developed by the Smithsonian Resident Associates. Our competition tests accuracy and catching ability, but does not reward long range throws as the Australians do; this serves to keep out the potentially perilous weighted boomerangs used by the Aussies to get extreme range and the bonus points that go with distance in competitions down under.*

BOOMERANG COMPETITION RULES
Smithsonian Resident Associates

This competition tests accuracy of throwing and ability to catch the boomerang upon its return. Large, heavy boomerangs are not permitted.

1. Contestants may make warm-up throws in a separate area immediately before making scoring throws.
2. Each contestant is permitted one practice throw in the scoring area to test the wind.
3. Competitors throw from anywhere inside a circle eight yards in diameter, with a marked center point.
4. The boomerang must be thrown outward a minimum of fifteen yards.
5. The throw must be judged an authentic boomerang throw.
6. Each contestant will make five scoring throws (or fewer, or more, depending on the size of the entry); number of throws allowed to be announced.
7. When the boomerang returns, a catch taken with one foot on the center point of the circle scores *ten* points; a catch taken with one foot inside the circle or on the line scores *seven* points; and a catch anywhere outside the circle scores *five* points. Touching the boomerang but not catching it with one foot on the center scores *three* points; a touch inside the circle *two* points; and a touch outside the circle *one* point.

---

*If you want a copy of Boomerang Association of Australia tournament rules, write to Ralph Sinclair, 3 Biscayne Drive, Syndal, Melbourne, Australia. He's an official of the group and will be glad to oblige.

66

8. Each throw must be made within twenty seconds of taking position, unless the judge permits more time.

9. Play-offs, if any, will immediately follow conclusion of the tournament.

10. Awards will be made when the throwing is completed.

If you want to expand the tournament, add other competitions: throwing to the peg and consecutive catching are ideal. The latter works best if the contestants form a long line, returning to the end of the line if they're still in the contest, and dropping out if they're not.

Tournaments are especially nice if you have a workshop a week or two earlier so people can make their own boomerangs. Participants should bring tools—pocketknives, rasps, planes, files, sandpaper, etc. Hand out precut plywood blanks (anyone with power equipment can make them from patterns provided in this book) that can be carved on the spot. Then have a short practice session to make sure all the creations work.

If you want to do any of this indoors, you might be able to show appropriate films from the Australian Information Service, which offers its films free to nonprofit organizations. For information, write to them at 636 Fifth Avenue, New York, New York. *Boomerang*, an attractive three minute color film of an Australian championship tournament, makes a hit with viewers. In the past, I've also borrowed from the Service an ethnological movie called *The Boomerang*. It shows an aborigine chopping down a tree and then crafting his own weapon. The twelve-minute film shows lots more of aboriginal life, including a great naked dance.

The thing to remember in all of this is that boomerang throwing is for fun. If more than one person is involved, you'll probably end up competing—after all, you're human —but you don't have to have rules and regulations to do it.

To establish a nice rhythm for the sport, take turns throwing boomerangs. Or try throwing around a boomerang-eating tree. Or at a tethered balloon. Let birds alone; they're nice to have around, and they'll easily dodge a boomerang, anyway.

If you are all good throwers and *if* you are all using light boomerangs that won't hurt anybody, you can play "Suicide," the traditional finale to boomerang sessions at the Ruhest, my family's farm in Pennsylvania, where everyone —residents, guests, and anyone else who wanders in—is more or less freakish for the sport. Everybody lines up and throws his boomerang on command. The object is to catch your own and duck everyone else's. A dozen boomerangs decorating the sky at one time is a noble sight, and the eye-and-hand coordination required to pluck yours out of the air while avoiding the rest separates the brave and skillful from the clumsy and cowardly.

A FLY-PAST OF BOOMERANGS

Boomerangs can be made of various materials: wood, plastic—even metal, if you want to create a flying knife. And they can be formed in a variety of shapes: the familiar sickle curve is customary, but boomerangs can also be made with three, four, and six blades; they can be shaped like the letters X, V, S, T, U, H, Y, and probably some of the rest of the alphabet. Aerodynamically, there is no difference. The essential thing is the cross section of the arms, which should be curved on one side and flat on the other.

Experimenting with boomerangs of different sizes, weights, and designs enhances the sport, so this chapter presents plans for boomerangs that are a bit different from the usual. The models range from indoor ones of cardboard and balsa wood to Herb Smith's weighted distance-record boomerang, from multi-bladers to a competition boomerang in the odd hook shape.

Once you get the feel for making and throwing boomerangs, you'll be able to invent your own designs. I have an acquaintance in the Washington, D.C. area who is working at perfecting a returning boomerang from a wooden coat hanger. He has succeeded in making the object circle halfway around before it dies; the last time I saw him, he vowed that with a little more experimentation he'd have it coming all the way back. I believe him.

The Cross Stick

Cross-stick boomerangs are the easiest of all to make, and they are guaranteed performers. There's even an aboriginal precedent for them, although few people know it. Fourbladers were used hundreds of years ago in what is now Queensland, along the northeast coast of Australia. One antique example collected in the nineteenth century (now on display in the British Museum's Department of Ethnography) had been used as a plaything by aboriginal boys.

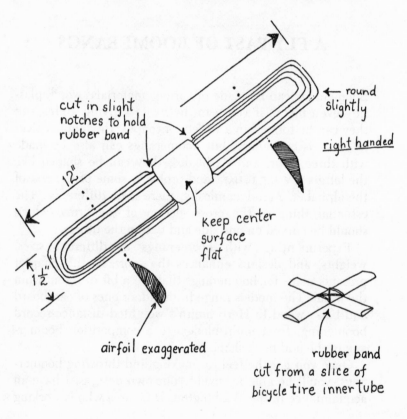

cut in slight notches to hold rubber band

← round slightly

right handed

12"

Keep center surface flat

1½"

airfoil exaggerated

rubber band cut from a slice of bicycle tire inner tube

1/ If you can get your hands on two plastic one-foot rulers with holes already drilled in the middle, you can make a workable cross-stick boomerang in as little as ten seconds. Just fasten the rulers together with a two-inch toggle bolt, or a bolt with a wing nut (to permit easy tightening after a hard landing has loosened it). Go to the nearest park or field, and launch it just as you would any other boomerang. It works surprisingly well.

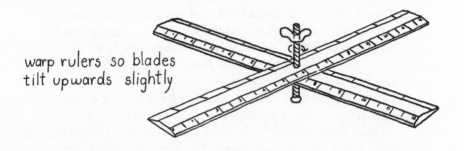

warp rulers so blades
tilt upwards slightly

2/ An indoor version of the cross stick can be made with balsa wood. Don't thin the edges down too much, or they'll nick when the boomerang lands. Attach the wings with glue or with strong rubber bands.

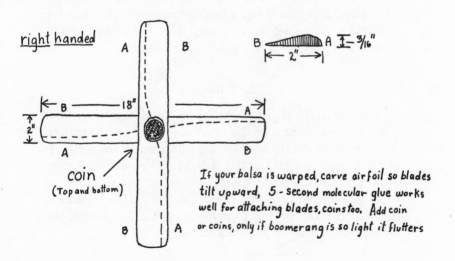

right handed

coin
(Top and bottom)

If your balsa is warped, carve airfoil so blades tilt upward, 5 - second molecular glue works well for attaching blades, coins too. Add coin or coins, only if boomerang is so light it flutters

71

3/ For a sturdy, high-performance outdoor cross stick, try using plywood. Get a good quality of exterior plywood (plywood made with glue that is not water-soluble) 3/16" thick. For the plan shown, cut the plywood to a 1 1/2" width and a 12" length. Carve the airfoil as indicated, cut notches to hold the rubber bands, and round the tips slightly. Fasten with a strong rubber band.

Make a number of these cross sticks at one time, numbering the faces so you know which fits on top after testing to determine which way each boomerang flies best. While you're at it, you can also alter lengths and widths to get a wider variety of boomerangs.

Painting your four-bladers adds to their beauty in flight. For a flashy effect, put stripes at the wing tips.

These boomerangs don't break easily because the rubber band acts as a shock absorber. But if an arm does break, you can always make the thing into a T-stick. Be aware that while you can make much larger cross sticks, the bigger ones can give you quite a crack on the knuckles on their return; their inertia increases rapidly with size. Double the size, and the boomerang cracks you four times as hard.

While the cross stick is easy to make and performs well, its drawback is that it has a less interesting flight than the customary two-wing boomerang. The cross stick whirls back and settles down in a predictable pattern.

The Pinwheel

A slow, graceful flight is the hallmark of this six-blader. The pinwheel is among the most accurate of boomerangs, floating home gently and settling into your hands softly. It is a pleasure to watch and a delight to throw. Depending on weight and range, it may be perfect for indoor throwing in an auditorium or gymnasium. The pinwheel's steadiness in flight is a function of its many wings; if one warps, the others compensate to maintain stability.

72

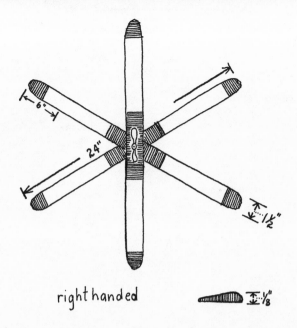

right handed

Pinwheels come in many sizes, but a nice one to make for indoor throwing uses three sticks of plywood (or wood such as basswood or tulip) 1/8" thick, 1 1/2" wide, and 24" long. Make one side convex by rasping, planing, or sanding it down. Then mark each stick inward six inches from each tip, and, placing the flat side six inches above a candle, bend each tip upward slightly. Now assemble them in the center with a toggle bolt or a bolt having a wing nut. Test fly it. If all has gone well, finish sanding it and then paint, shellac, or varnish it.

For outdoor flying, pinwheels can be made much heavier. An excellent long-range model can be constructed of sticks 36" long, 1 3/4" wide, and 1/2" thick. For strength, leave the sticks unbeveled in the center.

A Miniature Cardboard Boomerang

This boomerang is simplicity itself. With scissors, cut the boomerang out of a stiff card, such as a used playing card, a file card, or a cardboard folder. Three to six inches in length is about right, and any reasonable banana shape will do. Now bend up a wing tip as shown. Place it on a book for launching, and flick it sharply with a pencil or a finger.

73

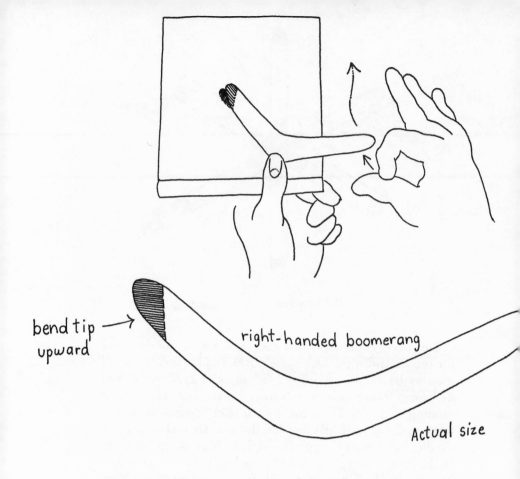

bend tip → upward

right-handed boomerang

Actual size

Tilt the book to find the best launch angle. The boomerang should go out three or four feet, curve around, and volplane back to the launch spot. This is fun in a classroom when the teacher is out of the room.

The "Bluey" Williams Hook

This is a scaled-down version of the original King Billy's Hook—the reduced size makes it easier to catch. The design is by the late "Bluey" Williams of Melbourne, one of the best competition-throwers in Australia, and maker of some fine boomerangs. This boomerang can be weighted with coins to increase its range. Use 3/8" plywood of the best quality.

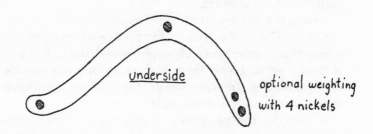

underside

optional weighting
with 4 nickels

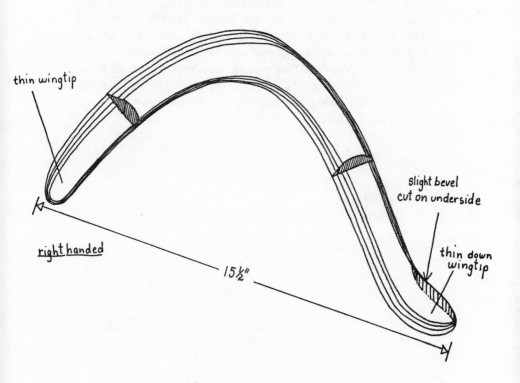

thin wingtip

right handed

slight bevel
cut on underside

thin down
wingtip

15½"

Herb Smith's Super Long-Range Boomerang

Using a boomerang of nine-ply birch plywood made from this plan, Smith achieved a well-documented throw of 108 yards out, with a return.

Notice the inner pattern superimposed on the outline of the plan. This is the area on the surface of the boomerang where the rasping away of surplus wood stops. Sandpaper is then used to blend these high spots into the surface of the boomerang. In other words, the sections are rounded, rather than having a steep angle.

A note on the weighting. Smith tries out each model with the weights strapped to the boomerang. If it performs well, he makes suitably shaped lead plugs and inserts these into holes drilled through the blades. He fits them flush with the blade or leaves them slightly above the surface and gives them a dome shape with taps of a hammer.

Smith emphasizes two points: the importance of using the very best quality birch plywood available and the importance of getting the balance point just right. This improves the flight.

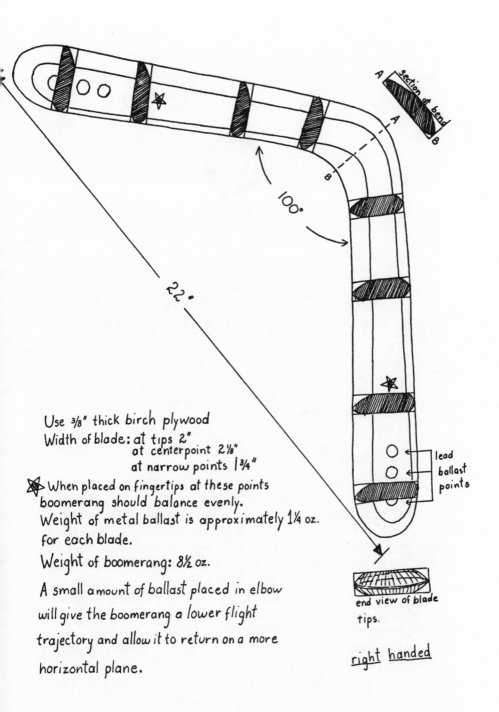

100°

22"

A — section of bend — A
B

B

Use ⅜" thick birch plywood
Width of blade: at tips 2"
          at centerpoint 2⅛"
          at narrow points 1¾"
⭐ When placed on fingertips at these points
boomerang should balance evenly.
Weight of metal ballast is approximately 1¼ oz.
for each blade.
Weight of boomerang: 8½ oz.

A small amount of ballast placed in elbow
will give the boomerang a lower flight
trajectory and allow it to return on a more
horizontal plane.

lead
ballast
points

end view of blade
tips.

right handed

TRANSMUTED BY BOOMERANG TO
TASTY KANGAROO MERINGUE

We've considered the charming, eccentric, returning boomerang. What about its close relative, the non-returning boomerang, or throw stick?

A weapon, such as a gun, capable of taking effect at a distance of 150 yards, is fascinating. The throw stick would customarily be used at much closer range, though. Aerodynamically, it's interesting, too, since it's actually more difficult to construct a throw stick that will fly in an undeviating straight line than it is to build a returning boomerang. Simply from the standpoint of cultural importance, the non-returner is worthy of study, since it was a basic Stone Age tool of those peoples who, over the millennia, roamed semi-desert regions around the world.

Ballistically, the flight path of the throw stick is more like that of modern bullets than any other Stone Age missile, arrows included. While the device flies reasonably fast, its real impact comes from its spin. A twelve-ounce, thirty-inch throw stick can stun or break the bones of animals at substantial distances. I want to emphasize this point—non-returners are potentially dangerous and must be treated with due respect. Take warning.

As I mentioned before, throw sticks existed in many places outside Australia—probably on every continent. It hasn't been documented yet, but I expect they'll even be discovered in places like the treeless pampas of South America and the steppes of central Asia. They're still being used today in parts of Australia and in the southwestern United States. Throw sticks are not very specialized weapons, so it's quite likely that they were invented in different places at different times without cross-cultural contacts.

How does a throw stick differ from a returning boomerang? To review, the typical non-returner is heavier, longer, has less angle between the arms (it has a banana shape, as opposed to the returner's crescent shape). It is launched horizontally, or nearly so, as compared with the nearly vertical launch for the returner. And it lacks that certain proportion of lift, weight, and angle between wings that permits the returner to home back to the thrower. The throw stick, though, as you shall see, is almost as interesting a device as its probable offspring and offers its own intriguing complexities. For some, it will be at least as challenging an object for experimentation.

Materials for Making Your Own

You can use modern power tools to make a throw stick; if you're determined to be authentic, you can use primitive stone tools. I'm opting for the middle ground as a nice compromise—modern hand tools.

The ideal material is marine or aircraft plywood 5/16" to 1/2" thick. These plywoods are expensive, but they're dense and hard. Standard five-ply plywood will do in a pinch, but it's a little light. The more weight you can pack in a given diameter, the farther you can throw your non-returner. Masonite is also very good; use waterproof, tempered, oil-impregnated boards at least 1/4" thick. For the necessary thickness, laminate several sheets together with resin glue.

It's far more challenging, though, to use curved limbs,

roots, or tree crotches in the primitive manner. You can sometimes find them in city lots being cleared for construction; in the country, look for sharply curved saplings growing from the steep banks of streams or cliffs and from rock outcroppings. Windblown areas like seacoasts and mountaintops may yield appropriately curved trunks or limbs; and they can also be found along steep-sided hills. Look for an angle of from 120° to 145°; 135° is optimum.

Don't use branches with knots in the curve; maximum strength is needed at the midpoint of a throw stick, and knots are weak points. You'll want to find a section that will produce a blank at least two inches wide; closer to three inches is even better. Material can always be cut away, but you can't add thickness.

There are many suitable American trees. Among them are the apple, buckeye, cherry, dogwood, elm, holly, sugar maple, mesquite, oak, persimmon, redbud, and sycamore. The honey locust and the yellow locust are also suitable and are particularly apt since they are close relatives of the acacia, one of the woods preferred by Australian aborigines for making throw sticks and boomerangs.

The denser, heavier, and harder the wood in your throw stick, the stronger it will be. It will break less easily, and it can be thrown greater distances. You should cut your wood in winter, when the sap is down. To avoid splitting and warping, season it slowly for about a month in a dry place outdoors. If the wood is green, submerging it under water is one way to quick-season it. This process removes the sap without dehydrating the pores. When you dry it, there is less chance of splitting and warping.

If you're working with plywood, use a handsaw or a coping saw for cutting your blank. If you're chopping down and roughing out blanks from saplings and tree limbs, use a sharp machete or a small ax. For shaping and finishing, you'll need a curved-surface rasp (the Shurform is an effective wood rasp), a metal scraper with ninety-degree edges, and sandpaper. These days the Australian aborigines use a small ax, a metal adz, and a piece of glass to make their boomerangs. Formerly, of course, they used stone and shell tools.

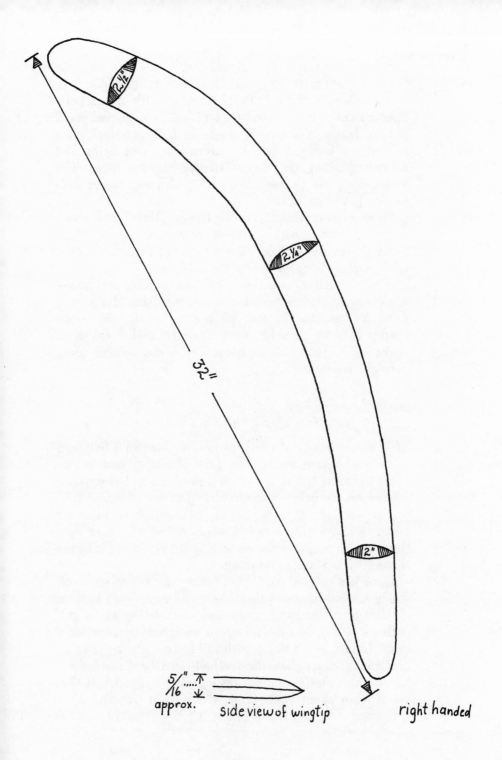

2½"

2¼"

2"

32"

5/16" approx.

side view of wingtip

right handed

If you have just a little experience, it will take you only ten or fifteen minutes to cut down and rough out a two-and-a-half-inch thick limb or sapling with a machete. Spend another twenty minutes on it with a rasp, and you'll have a blank in the right shape—a half-inch-thick cross section much like a double-convex lens. Test flying and further finishing take about twenty minutes more. The whole thing can be done in an hour, although power tools obviously will speed things up.

To seal out moisture, give the finished throw stick several good rubdowns with oil, tallow, or wax, or else varnish it. Later on, as the surface becomes dented from use, you'll find yourself doing on-the-spot refinishing.

If you launch it correctly—with suitable force and spin—a well-made, finely tuned non-returner should fly in a more or less straight line for approximately 100 yards. Flights of more than 150 yards are rare; and if you get a flight longer than 200 yards on a calm day, you're doing very well indeed!

Test Flying and Fine Tuning

After you've roughed out your non-returner to a flattened shape and before you do the final finishing, take it outdoors for some test throws. You'll need a windless day and a large empty field—a football field or a golf course fairway is just right. It saves a lot of walking to have a partner along to throw your *wunkun* back. Above all, make sure there are no people in range—when out of control, a heavy throw stick is a dangerous thing.

Until you're used to it, don't toss your throw stick full strength. Non-returners that aren't well tuned may hook to the left or to the right at the end of their flights, as golf balls do, and they can end up in some very strange locations. In fact, don't throw with full force until you're in an area much larger than the football-sized field needed for test flights. The reason for testing on a calm day is that you'll learn about your throw stick's flight patterns; after it's tuned, you can throw when it's breezy. With a little help from the wind you'll get some spectacular flights.

When you're testing, imagine that you're holding a sickle. If it is symmetrical, hold your non-returner by either end, with its hook pointing forward. Throw it sidearm; the plane of the axis should be parallel to the ground. Give it plenty of wrist snap when you let go. Throw it gently, then harder, until you have a good picture of its flight pattern. You may find that it curves to the left (rarely) or right (more commonly). If it curves to the right, try a three-quarters overhand throw. This is the way many Australian aborigines launch. Sometimes you can improve flights by changing the end you hold when you throw, although you'll probably settle on a favorite end rather quickly.

An aerodynamically correct non-returner will fly in a straight line if it is thrown horizontally or almost horizontally. Less perfect ones can be made to work almost as well by changing the launch. On flights that curve to the right, use the three-quarter-overhand throw I've described (tilting the end up). This produces a flight in the shape of an elongated S, that is so beautiful you might prefer to throw this way all the time. If you want a straight-line trajectory, you'll be doing lots of fine tuning, and you'll need some luck too; all the delicate variables that produce perfect flights have yet to be explored.

Take your rasp or scraper along when you're test flying so you can make adjustments on the spot. Plane down the top or bottom sides (or both) of each limb until you get the flight pattern you want. Rasping at the bottom corner of the leading edge will increase lift. Making an approximate convex-plano section (upper side flatter, lower side more curved) will reduce lift. If the throw stick is too thick, plane each face evenly. It's best to start with a non-returner about 1/2" thick, thinning it down to about 3/8" during the test session.

Australian aborigines often use a different method for setting the trim on their weapons' arms: they shape the limbs into a plano-convex cross section (curved upper surface, flat lower surface) that looks like the cross section of an airplane wing and produces a similar lift. Be aware, however, that too much lift is a disadvantage; a high-climbing throw stick is not what you're aiming for.

Another aboriginal alternative is planing down the non-returner limbs until they're so thin there is no effective lift from air foil—lift will be obtained another way. The limb tips are gently heated, and the two edges that cut into the air as the boomerang spins are twisted into an upward skew to increase their "bite." It is this bite that produces lift. To visualize what the boomerang looks like if viewed down its length, imagine a propellor. Another way to visualize the process is to get a yardstick or another such flat, bendable object. Hold it by the ends. Now twist your left hand clockwise, your right hand counterclockwise. That's the skew.

The process, of course, works in reverse. If the boomerang has too much lift and is climbing too high for your taste, you can curb this by reversing the twisting. Make the tip ends of the leading edges skew downwards as much as needed.

A second type of bending is customary and much easier to accomplish. This is the imparting of an upward twist at both wing tips, to create what is called a positive or upward dihedral. Looked at head on, it appears a wide-angled vee, thus ($\wedge$). The dihedral angle adds stability and is found in the set of both bird and aircraft wings. Likewise, helicopter blades are made flexible enough to bend upwards at the tips as they whirl around, thus making the craft fly with greater equilibrium.

To do heat tuning right at the test site, get a fire going. Heat the limbs over coals, not flames, to prevent scorching, and hold the arm three to four inches above the coals for a couple of minutes. The throw stick should be a little too hot to touch with your bare hands. Wearing gloves for protection, twist the limb in the direction you want, and hold it there until it's cool. You can skew the limb between closely growing saplings if there are any around. Or carry a forked stick, and twist the limb between the forks.

You can do the same thing at home with a 400-degree oven. In the winter, you can insert the throw stick between the bars of an old-fashioned radiator and twist the arms.

So, to sum up, there are three ways to modify a non-returner's flight patterns: 1/ You can replace surfaces to

make them more lenticular, more plano-convex, more convex-plano, or thinner; 2/ you can twist the leading edges of the arms up or down by heating them; 3/ using heat, you can bend the limb tips up or down to increase or decrease the dihedral angle. The solution varies with the throw stick.

The best bet is to give your weapon a lenticular cross section with no upward or downward dihedral angle and no wing tip skew, and work from there. This should produce a serviceable non-returning boomerang with a satisfactory flight pattern. Then you can tinker all you want.

Repair

Throw sticks land hard, and damage is inevitable. Use epoxy glue to repair cracks, and clamp the pieces together until they are dry. After that, scrape or sand the cracked area as needed. Test fly it to see how the flight pattern has been modified—bonded throw sticks rarely keep their original flight patterns. If you're lucky, you might get an even better performance. But be careful: even if you've used epoxy, your implement won't be as strong as it was.

Errett Callahan is a doctoral candidate at the American University in Washington, D.C. He's one of the new breed of anthropologists who try to understand primitive cultures by re-enacting their lifestyles—reconstructing the tools used by the people, and living as they lived. As part of his work, he has experimented extensively with throw sticks.

His best distance-throwing session was at the Flint Run Paleo-Indian archaeological site near Front Royal, Virginia. He threw with Robert Gillum of Raleigh, North Carolina, and they used a twenty-six-inch-long throw stick made of sourwood; it weighed seven ounces, had a lenticular cross section, and a curve of 135 degrees.

"All afternoon we threw back and forth, up and down the meadow," Callahan reports. "Robert, a huge man [Callahan himself is six-feet-three and strongly built, with a powerful throwing arm] got flights of up to 190 yards. My best distance was 170. The throw stick was so finely tuned that we got virtual straight-line flights with no noticeable deviation to the right or left. We threw the throw stick with its limbs parallel to the ground, or maybe tilted up a fraction. The flights stayed a constant three to five feet above the ground until near the very end; the throw stick flew in a spectacular beeline, rotating like a propellor all the way. The distances we threw that day remain our best to date, although we do think a slightly heavier non-returner would have given us throws longer than 200 yards."

Callahan estimated these distances, but they're probably pretty accurate. He has trained himself to make a one-yard pace; I've seen him do it and have measured the step myself.

Callahan has tried hunting too. He took a group of students to northern Arizona to recreate the life of an Indian desert band of 5,000 years ago. For twenty days they stayed at basalt quarries, making replicas of stone tools, foraging for greens, berries, seeds, and cacti, and hunting and trapping animals for meat. As you might expect, the pickings were slim. They bagged a number of ground squirrels with bows and arrows made with their stone tools. But the rabbits were elusive.

Still, Callahan found the futile rabbit hunts instructive. "We learned that the use of a rabbit stick [a small throw stick] in hunting required a clear area between thrower and quarry. But we needed cover to stalk wary prey, and jackrabbits are wary! The most feasible way to do this was to use the Indian trick of holding a leafy branch to break the body outline, moving forward only when the rabbit was looking the other way. By walking so your movement was no more than the wind in the bushes, you can cut the chances of being seen to a minimum. Using this technique we approached to within twenty to twenty-five yards of our prey several times—sometimes, in the early evening, without having to use branches.

"When I thought I was as close as a particular animal would allow me to get I assumed a throwing position (standing with the left foot forward, facing the animal), brought my arm back slowly, then threw hard with as quick and as minimal a body movement as feasible. I counted on wrist snap, not only to propel the missile forward with maximum rotation, but also to reduce body movement. Only rarely did I see a rabbit move before the rabbit stick landed; they don't seem to see the danger quickly enough. With two rabbit sticks, you sometimes can get in more than one throw, especially if your first is thrown too high and lands some distance away.

"I've hit to the right and hit to the left and whipped overhead and thrown dirt in the faces of many rabbits, but I still haven't hit one. This, it must be noted, is due to my lack of proficiency and practice in accurate throwing. Without too much more practice than I have had, one should have a better than 50 per-cent chance of hitting a rabbit-sized target at twenty yards. The throw stick has to come within only a foot or so of the target horizontally to make contact, since its rotating limbs cut a slice through the air as wide as the boomerang is long. Naturally, practice in throwing at targets and in stalking are prerequisites for successful hunts."

Callahan's experiments haven't been complete failures. Here's his happy ending: "Now that I think of it, I did bag an animal once with a returning boomerang. I was throwing it at twilight when a bat came flittering into the meadow. Wondering how he might react to a bat-like flying companion, I threw the boomerang into the air. To my surprise, he ducked as it went by, but on the return flight, as it approached the ground he dove down, narrowly missing the boomerang, and crashed into the ground, knocking himself unconscious. I was tempted to take him back to camp as my first kill. But how could I say I brought home the bacon when the bacon was hunting the boomerang?"

ODDS AND ENDINGS

Where Can I Find Them?

If you haven't actually seen any boomerangs, the place to go is a natural history museum. They can sometimes be found in air and space museums, too. There may be only a few on display, but most institutions with an interest in ethnology or aeronautics have good study collections in storage. Often you can see these research collections by appointment. If approached in a scholarly way, museum people tend to be enormously obliging. It's much easier to get behind the scenes than you think.

There are several good American collections. The Smithsonian Institution's Museum of Natural History holds dozens of Australian throw sticks and boomerangs and several hundred rabbit sticks from the southwestern United States. The National Air and Space Museum, also part of the Smithsonian, has boomerangs, too, since its curators are interested in complex aerodynamic principles. The collection is in two parts: the first was put together at the turn of the century by flight theorist Samuel Langley, and the second is a contemporary collection that I'm assembling for the museum, containing both aboriginal specimens and the best of modern commercial boomerangs. Included as well are a number used to set world's records.

The American Museum of Natural History in New York has a handsome display of Australian boomerangs on view. The Field Museum, in Chicago, has a study collection focusing on Hopi rabbit sticks—whose original value is evident from the careful sinew bindings of those that had been cracked down the middle from one hard landing too many. Universities such as Pennsylvania, Harvard, Yale, and Berkeley are among the many other places around the country where you can search out boomerangs.

For those with a penchant for solving mysteries, the collection at the British Museum's Department of Ethnography holds an attraction. Their records were either lost or destroyed at the turn of the century, reportedly by an insane curator. Visiting experts are invited to write comments on interesting specimens, as the museum would like to compile new documentation. Cambridge University's museum has a boomerang collection, as does Oxford's Ashmolean, which also owns the records of Howard Carter's Egyptian tomb finds.

England, curiously enough, may be a better place to buy antique Australian aboriginal throw sticks and boomerangs than Australia. Englishmen returning from Australia in the last 150 years brought boomerangs home as souvenirs. In Australia, the supply has been snapped up by collectors.

On the Continent, there are museum collections in Paris, Florence, Leiden, Hanover, Cologne, Munich, and Leipzig. One of the greatest troves, that of a Hamburg museum, was destroyed during World War II. In Egypt, the Cairo Museum is the home of some of the most ancient throw sticks—those of the royal tombs.

Not surprisingly, Australia has the mother lode. The South Australian Museum owns more than six thousand throw sticks and boomerangs, including dozens of the curious "prestige boomerangs" from the Cooper's Creek area. Another of their treasures is a single Egyptian Twentieth Dynasty tomb throw stick, so delicate and so valuable no curator has ever had the nerve to throw it. Norman Tindale, curator emeritus there, thinks it would work pretty well, and that it might possibly even return.

There are fairly rich collections in the National Museum, Melbourne; the Australian Museum, Sydney; the Western Australian Museum, Perth; the Queensland Museum, Brisbane; the Tasmanian Museum, Hobart; and the Insitute of Anatomy, in Canberra. Some private collections, it is believed, may rival those of the museums.

Beef baron Tom McCourt, of Beechport, South Australia, is one of the most interesting private collectors. He's taken his traveling laboratory all over the country in pursuit of his ethnographic studies. McCourt gave me a report on the 1967 find of many aboriginal implements, including boomerangs, when a water hole in the Bulloo River near Bulloo Downs Station went dry. Tools found buried in the mud there were fairly well preserved and are known to be more than a century old.

There's also a mystery collection, supposedly of thousands of throw sticks and boomerangs, gathered by one of the first settlers of the Wellington area of New South Wales. The story is that he traded "white man's goods" such as tea, flour, and tobacco to aborigines in return for boomerangs. Then he tossed them into the eaves of a woodshed, where they have sat for generations, awaiting rediscovery. The man who told me this tale added that the whole thing may be a "purphy," Cockney slang for rumor. He pointed out in his scholarly way that purphy can also be spelled "furfy."

Good and Bad, Big and Little Boomerangs

The very best commercial returning boomerang of them all? It all depends what you want to do with it. But one nominee is the Comeback, manufactured in Germany. The maker is Willi Urban, of Leutershausen, Bavaria. He constructs his boomerangs of nylon, with fiberglass re-inforcing and advertises them as virtually unbreakable and unwarpable.

It's easy to believe his boomerangs are strong. Dan Galo,

91

of Brunswick, Ohio, neatly took off a car aerial with his. A Washingtonian wrecked the fender of a Volkswagen (internecine touch, that) with his. Pearre Chase, of Bryan, Texas, used his boomerang to score a lucky hit and deter a big dog from chasing his little poodle. "The owner thought it was a mad bird," reported Chase.

Peril to man and beast, the Comeback must *always* be thrown with the greatest caution.

Just the opposite is a curiosity in my collection, a multi-armed Orbiteer of plastic. Distributed as a company promotion years ago by the Standard Oil Company of California, the six-blader, with arms attached to a circular rim, is easy to toss and easy to catch. Considering that tens of thousands were in circulation, it's interesting that the Standard Oil people had to do a lot of searching to come up with a single specimen for the Smithsonian. It's like the World War II Army dress hats that have glutted the market, while fatigue hats produced in the multi-millions are exceedingly rare.

Another charmer in my collection is a little red and white four-blader, exceedingly well crafted, from the late Colonel John Gerrish, of Portland, Oregon. A lawyer by trade, Gerrish was long fascinated by boomerangs and manufactured them for years. Combining business with pleasure, he would peddle his boomerangs when he traveled. Stopping in a village in the Midwest for gas, he went to the grocery store nearby. "Want any boomerangs?" he asked. "Nope," said the proprietor. "Got a whole box of them in the back. Been there for years." Gerrish hastened back. What he found was a dusty box full of boomerangs never taken from their packets, made by the Brist Manufacturing Company, of Topeka, Kansas, and with a patent date of 1902.

Gerrish acquired the whole box. He was pleased to note that buyers of the boomerangs were urged to send for the rules of a boomerang game, and to enclose a two-cent stamp for postage. Those were the days.

Literature enclosed with these boomerangs claimed:

"The Brist boomerang . . . will go down in history as the most wonderful novel invention of the age . . . anyone can, with but little practice, do [with] it such incredulous things, that were you to have appeared among your friends for half an hour's entertainment a century ago, you would duly have been tried and convicted of witchcraft."

For spectacular, long-range flights, one of the best of all boomerangs is the King Billy's Hook made by "Bluey" Williams, a red-haired Melbourne postman. (With perverse humor, Australians call redheads "Bluey.")

Separating fact from fancy is hard, but the story is that the original King Billy was an aborigine who lived in Melbourne around the turn of the century and owned a curious hook-shaped boomerang. In recent years, the design was copied by competition throwers in that area, who then whipped everyone in sight with their creations. The original shape is a sort of rounded-off figure seven, and the boomerang measures seventeen inches across; in Williams' version and in others I've seen, the shape becomes more of a question mark, and the size diminishes to about eleven inches. Weights are added to increase the range.

The ones Williams made for me had two-penny pieces bedded at the wing tips and one bedded at the center. Requiring the hardest throw you can give them, they go sailing out long and low, come flying back still low, and virtually die as they arrive home, so they are easy to catch. They're perfect for competitions where points are given for distance, accuracy, and catching.

I once threw the one "Bluey" had inscribed "To All Smithsonians" for National Geographic Society photographer Joe Goodwin, and as it disappeared in the distance, he said: "Well, you lost that one." But the boomerang turned and came sailing back, and I caught it easily within twenty feet of the launching point. Goodwin just shook his head.

I have in my collection a five-footer of lancewood from Mornington Island, east of Arnhem Land. A recent newsclip from Australia reported that a police sergeant went to the island to investigate a complaint and was felled by a boomerang. Stitches were required to repair the damage to his head. With apologies to the sergeant, I must say that my big Mornington Island boomerang now pleases me even more.

At the other extreme, I own what may be the world's smallest workable boomerang—a three-inch model made of formed styrofoam. It is launched by spring from the side of an ashtray, flies out about four feet, then circles back to land, scattering the ashes nicely. My friends declare it a great time-waster. "By the way," several have inquired, "could you get one of them for me?"

For all-around excellence, the various boomerangs made by Lorin Hawes, at Mudgeeraba, Queensland, are unbeatable. Fun and easy for a novice to manage, they challenge the most adept thrower as well. His basic boomerangs are the M17, a seventeen-inch model of marine plywood; the Super Looper, a smaller version of the M17; and the Silky Spinner, a creation of silky oak spliced together at the center for strength. With its hand-rubbed finish, this is a connoisseur's boomerang. A Silky Spinner for a time was my favorite boomerang, then I broke it into four pieces, and grieved. Not for long. Glued back together, it worked even better than before. The dynamic balance had accidentally been improved.

Hawes, incidentally, was involved in what may be the funniest moment in boomerang history. A few years ago an aboriginal senator attempted to make it illegal for anyone but an aborigine to manufacture boomerangs in Australia, and thus cash in on the lucrative curio business for tourists. A controversy naturally developed. As an expatriate American manufacturing boomerangs for a living, Hawes was drawn in. He challenged the legislator to a throw-off; the senator was to use boomerangs of his own manufacture while Hawes came with boomerangs he had made. The legislator refrained from a challenge match before assembled press, but did give a demonstration. When one of his boomerangs landed in a tree, he was forced to shinny up to retrieve it—with television cameras duly recording the spectacle.

Unworkable, expensive, trashy boomerangs are all over the place. Try most any American sporting goods store. Australia has the plague too; unworkable boomerangs are produced in the tens of thousands for visitors to take home as curiosities.

I bought an Italian boomerang that comes complete with instructions on how to catch it. An aerodynamic joke, it doesn't have a ghost of a chance of ever returning. A sixty-nine-cent Japanese creation purchased, of all unlikely places, in a curio shop on Virginia's Skyline Drive has completely unsanded edges. The boomerang goes out, starts to turn, then nosedives into the turf.

On the other hand, the red plastic Wham-O boomerang, made by the makers of the Frisbee, is a reasonable performer. It certainly is a good buy, although availability seems to be a problem. But good boomerangs are hard to find all around the world, even in Australia. My advice is to make your own from the plans in this book, analyze them, and invent your own variations. Therein lies the path of true satisfaction.

If you *must* buy your boomerangs ready made, write for a price list from Boomerang, Box 7324, Benjamin Franklin Station, Washington, D.C. 20044. This importer handles many of the world's best commercially made boomerangs.

Transport, or What Are You Carrying in the Funny-Looking Sack?

When you have several boomerangs, carrying them gets to be a problem because of their different curves and lengths. The easiest and cheapest solution is an old-fashioned string bag. But you can elaborate. I've had three different ones made for me by leatherworkers, each of whom came up with a different design.

One case is made of two triangles sewn together; it has a

snap to fasten it and a loop of leather to go over the shoulder. Another is shaped something like an archer's quiver, except that it's much bigger and has a slight curve at the top to accommodate the strange boomerang shape. Boomerangs—especially large ones—look beautiful in it, but it's quite difficult to carry since it tends to slap against your leg, slip off your shoulder, and, as it slides around, poke into your back.

The most elegant is a field case designed and crafted by Chuck Cuendet of Jackson, Mississippi, to hold twenty-five small boomerangs. The case and strap are made of hand-dyed harness leather; thirty-two feet of rawhide make up a braided lacing. Mississippi black walnut is used for strap anchors and for the latch that closes the case in front. Cuendet was so pleased with his creation that he exhibited it in the Mississippi Governor's Craft Exhibit, where, he writes, "it had a great many people musing over its unique purpose."

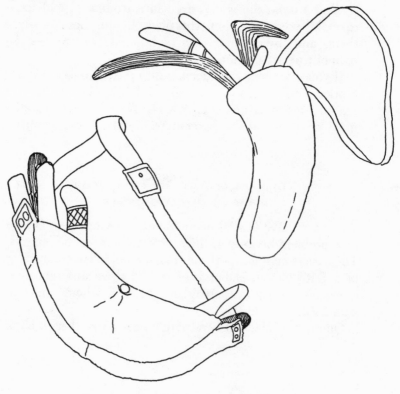

Boomerangs as UFOs

Some jurisdictions have laws against throwing things like extra-heavy, extra-large boomerangs, which might qualify as dangerous missiles. At one time you couldn't even fly a kite in Washington, and the 1892 law that proscribed it—and presumably boomerang throwing—is a good example of other laws you might run into: "It shall not be lawful for any person or persons within the District of Columbia to throw any stone or other missile in any street, avenue, alley, road, or highway, or open space, or public square, or inclosure under penalty of not more than five dollars for every such offense." Be warned. Be cautious when you throw. If the fine wouldn't hurt, the lawsuit would.

As a practical matter, ordinances like this don't come to much unless you happen to hit someone or something. What actually happens when you're throwing boomerangs is that an interested policeman politely inquires what's going on, carefully studies the situation, then says, "Can I try too?"

Satisfying Harmonies

People have been throwing boomerangs in America for years. I've talked to elderly men who remember playing with them as boys, and as it turns out, there are a number of boomerang patents dating from the turn of the century on file at the U.S. Patent Office. So why the fresh enthusiasm these days?

Consider the Frisbee, symbol of that decade of disenchantment, the 1960s. The appeal is much the same. Frisbees and boomerangs are space-age devices. Balls are ballistic missiles that travel in parabolas or curves. "The kids are tired of the ball," says Dr. Stancil Johnson, historian of the Frisbee phenomenon. "I am too. We've been playing with spheres so long, we're blind with them. All there is to a ball is the simple Newtonian discovery that if you throw it up, it will come down." That's not much compared to the complicated paths of Frisbees—and boomerangs—which have airfoils and can defy gravity.

Frisbees and boomerangs are anti-sport; they mock the

over-organized, over-commercialized world of professional athletics. Competitions are resolutely amateurish, which means very few rules and peculiar prizes.

Best of all, throwing either a Frisbee or a boomerang is a creative, individual activity. You can compete with them, of course, but their real beauty lies elsewhere, in what Frisbee fans call jamming—free-style throwing. Then the device and the body blend in surprising and satisfying harmonies.

Frisbees and boomerangs have the charm of simplicity; both actually are complex and unpredictable devices. Throwing tends to be abandoned and spontaneous, special delights we find all too rarely.

The Frisbee may now have had its day, and boomerangs may be too temperamental to become the darlings of Everyman. But the small disk and the flying delta wing are as good as any symbols I know for the thinker—the person who wants to be an individual in a complex, regimented, rule-filled world.

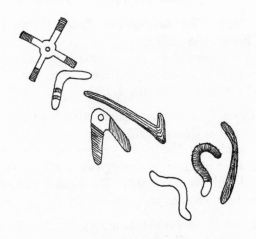

BIBLIOGRAPHY
ABOUT STICKS THAT FLY

There's substantial literature on throw sticks and boomerangs—both literary and journalistic—in a variety of languages. Beginning with the early explorers, the two devices have been treated in manners ranging from factual to fanciful, with the emphasis on the latter. Even scientific writing, particularly in the nineteenth century, tends to be rather muddled. But charm is rarely absent. Writers have names like Lane Fox (you'll often find him under *Pitt-Rivers*), and titles run to the exotic: "Savage Life in Central Australia," for example.

The following bibliography is a personal selection, emphasizing contemporary writing on the subject, some of it unpublished, but all of it reasonably available.

Only works in the English language are cited. The emphasis is on the returning boomerang.

If you desire a more complete bibliography, you are invited to consult one of several that have been published. For example, Felix Hess's list in his doctoral dissertation is fairly exhaustive, in more ways than one.

Books and Booklets

Hanson, M. J. *The Boomerang Book*. Harmondsworth: Penguin Books, Inc., 1974.

Writing for youngsters, Hanson manages to explain complex matters in a simple and interesting way. The price ($1.25 in the United States) is right.

Hawes, Lorin L. and Mary Ellen. *All About Boomerangs*. Sydney: Hamlyn Group, 1975.

In this profusely illustrated volume, the Haweses cover the whole subject of returning boomerangs. Their prose is a model of wit and clarity. The book is one of the two or three best writings on boomerangs.

Hawes, Lorin L., and Ruhe, Benjamin P. "The Boomerang." Washington, D.C.: The Smithsonian Institution, 1970.

Dr. Hawes is the author of portions of the text, and the author of this book is a contributor as well as the compiler of the work. Periodically revised, the booklet is issued in conjunction with the annual Smithsonian Resident Associates' boomerang workshop and tournament.

Hess, Felix. "Boomerangs: Aerodynamics and Motion." Privately printed. Groningen: 1975.

A 350-page dissertation by Dr. Hess for his doctoral degree in mathematics, this volume includes ethnographic information; general physical information on throw sticks and boomerangs; a bibliography of several hundred titles in several languages; mathematical theory; wind tunnel experiments in aerodynamics; theoretical flight paths; photographically recorded experimental flight paths; and many stereo pictures. This is the most comprehensive scientific study of the boomerang ever published.

Mannix, Daniel P. *A Sporting Chance: Unusual Methods of Hunting*. New York: E. P. Dutton, 1967.

In Chapter 7 of this book, "Boomerang: The Stick that Flies," the author recounts his rather unfruitful experience in hunting wary ducks with throw sticks. He also gives an eye-witness report of Hopi Indians using such weapons in a horseback chase of jackrabbits. For the sake of the dramatic, the account seems at times to give way to fancy.

Mason, Bernard S., *Boomerangs: How to Make and Throw Them*. New York: Dover Publications, 1974.
This is an unaltered republication of Part I, "Boomerangs," from *Primitive and Pioneer Sports* by Mason, originally published in 1937. It emphasizes multi-bladed boomerangs for children, and includes plans for three-bladed, four-bladed and six-bladed boomerangs. Treatment of traditional Australian boomerangs is perfunctory.

Smith, Herb A. *Boomerangs: Making and Throwing Them*. Littlehampton: Gemstar Publications, 1975.
A fine booklet on boomerangs, particularly interesting for Mr. Smith's boomerang construction plans. His information on making and throwing long-distance, weighted boomerangs is a unique contribution to the sport.

Urban, Willi. "The Sport-Boomerang 'Comeback.'" Privately printed. Leutershausen: West Germany, 1975.
Explaining how the nylon 'Comeback' boomerang he manufactures can best be thrown, Mr. Urban imparts considerable wisdom on the subject of boomerangs in general.

Periodicals

Burroughs, John. "How to Make a Boomerang." *Popular Science*, May 1956, pp. 225-28.
Gives a plan for a rather clumsy boomerang. Text is often fanciful (". . . the boomerang . . . spins 150 yards in a straight line . . . then it zooms upward to an altitude of more than 100 feet. . . ."). Some good action photographs.

Davidson, D. S. "Australian Throwing Sticks, Throwing Clubs, and Boomerangs." *American Anthropologist*, Vol. 38, pp. 76-100.
Davidson's conclusion on how boomerangs evolved is in-

teresting: "In a culture where throwing sticks undoubtedly have been in use for a great period of time, we do not have to look far for a possible as well as a most reasonable basis from which boomerangs could have been derived."

Hess, Felix. "The Aerodynamics of Boomerangs." *Scientific American*. November 1968, pp. 124-36.
This brilliant article alone fostered a small boom in boomerangs in several parts of the world. In England, for example, a direct outgrowth was the formation of the Society for the Promotion and Avoidance of Boomerangs. The first portion of the article is general and of interest to any reader; the second part, describing field experiments that test computer-assisted analysis of the forces that affect boomerang flight paths, is rather abstruse. Nicely illustrated.

Hess, Felix. "A Returning Boomerang From the Iron Age." *Antiquity*. Cambridge: St. John's College, December 1973.
Dr. Hess made a plywood duplicate of an oak boomerang dating from 300 B.C. that was unearthed in Holland. According to this careful article, his tests indicated that the original boomerang was capable of return flights.

James, Brennig. "Boomerang: Glassfibre Technique Applied to an Age-Old 'Flying Machine.'" *Aero Modeller* (England). January 1971, pp. 39-40.
A short illustrated article by an English physician and noted sailplane pilot. He seeks to improve boomerang performance through the use of fiber glass construction.

McCarthy, Frederick D. "Boomerangs." *Australian Encyclopedia*, pp. 44-45.
A concise, authoritative summary of the subject.

McCarthy, Frederick D. "The Boomerang," *The Australian Museum Magazine*. September 15, 1961, pp. 343-49.
A scholarly discussion of the history, types, geographical distribution, and uses of boomerangs and throw sticks.

Musgrove, Peter J. "Many Happy Returns." *New Scientist* (England), January 24, 1974, pp. 186-89.

Describes investigations into the flight of returning boomerangs conducted under the author's direction at the University of Reading. A mechanical boomerang launcher was constructed as part of this undergraduate project. This distinguished article is representative of the pioneering boomerang research now being done around the world by young scientists.

Musgrove, Peter J. "Prehistoric Aeronautics." *Hemisphere*, 1975.

Informed, intelligent speculation on how the boomerang came to be invented.

Pileggi, Sarah. "And Many Happy Returns," *Sports Illustrated*. New York: July 29, 1974.

A brief account of the first United States Open Boomerang Tournament. It nicely catches the low-keyed tone of this Smithsonian Institution Resident Associates' event on Washington's National Mall. Unusually pleasant reading. It concludes: "When you release that thing [boomerang]," said Bob Coakley, a somewhat portly gray-haired computer systems analyst, "you have pre-set into it about five different factors—forward thrust, elevation to the horizon, angle of the rotating plane, the provision you make for the wind, and the force you impart to the spinning. So you let go of the damn thing, and you stand back and watch it do all these things, and you think, my God, did I do that?"

Ruhe, Benjamin P. "The Art and Sport of Boomeranging." *Smithsonian*. Washington: August, 1970, pp. 49-51.

An account of the first Smithsonian Associates Boomerang Festival.

Smith, Frank. "The Boomerang." *Shell Aviation News*, No. 285, 1962, pp. 7-10.

A witty view of the literature—some of it esoteric—on boomerangs.

Stivens, Dal. "The Beauty of the Boomerang." *Mayfair*, May 1957.
Some boomerang lore, entertainingly told.

Stivens, Dal. "The Boomerang Is Booming." *Walkabout* (Australia), July 1963.
Discusses the revival of interest in boomerangs in Australia.

——, *Boomerang Bulletin*, newsletter of the Boomerang Association of Australia.
First issued in 1970. Reports periodically on competitions, prints articles on making and throwing boomerangs, etc. Write to Jim Robb, 14 Elliot Street, Knoxfield 3180, Australia.

——, *The Journal of the Society for the Promotion and Avoidance of Boomerangs.*
First issued in 1970. Reports at irregular intervals on activities of this British association and gives reports on boomerang construction, etc. Major Christopher Robinson, 12 Stoneham Close, Reading, Berks, England, is the editor. He welcomes correspondence.

Unpublished Papers

Callahan, Errett. "The Non-Returning Boomerang: Evolution and Experiment." Richmond, Virginia: Virginia Commonwealth University, 1975, 47 pages.
First-hand experiments leading to some convincing conclusions. Much of Chapter IX of this book is based on this paper.

Rayner, Gordon. "Boomerang Engineering," 60 pages, illustrated.
Done in connection with the writer's graduate research, this paper explores precession, dihedral, autorotation, left-hand symmetric boomerangs, and airfoils.

Robson, David. "The Boomerang." 1976, 52 pages.
This paper may well be the first comprehensive explanation for the layman of exactly why a boomerang returns. Every principle involved in the flight is explained in

terms easily understood by the careful reader. Clearly illustrated.

Tindale, Norman, "A Gathering of Australian Aboriginal Words for Boomerang." A nineteen-page manuscript in the possession of the author of this book. Given as a gift by Dr. Tindale.

As exemplified in his monumental *Aboriginal Tribes of Australia*, published in 1974 by Stanford University, Dr. Tindale feels that the detailed plotting of tribal distributions will more effectively explore the material culture, vocabulary, social patterns, behavior, and practice of Australian aborigines. His project has been in progress for fifty years. Well over half of the words in this test gathering of approximately 300 words applied to the non-returning and returning boomerang were freshly gathered from aboriginal sources and linked with specific tribal names. The balance came from the collation of older published sources. The relatively high degree of agreement between the results from the two types of sources (there was an overlap in at least a third of the cases), suggests a reasonable degree of accuracy in the rendering given. A master file card preserves the sources in detail. At the time of the gift of the list to the author in April 1975, Dr. Tindale noted, "My own studies, based on plotting data on maps and making personal interpretations of the distributions seen thereon, are proceeding."